Sprint 8
Cardio Protocol

Sprint-intensity cardio targeting exercise-induced growth hormone for a New You

by

Phil Campbell, M.S., M.A., FACHE, ACSM - CPT

2016

Second Printing 2017

www.Sprint8book.com
www.Sprint8.com
www.40speed.com
www.readysetgofitness.com
mail: info@Sprint8book.com
ISBN: 978-0-692-65002-8
Library of Congress Control Number: 2016903561

This book is designed to provide information in regard to the subject matter covered for healthy adults who have obtained physician clearance before beginning the Sprint 8 Cardio Protocol or any exercise program. This book is sold with the understanding that the publisher, author and advisors are not rendering medical advice or any other professional services. An examination by a physician needs to be performed BEFORE attempting to begin the Sprint 8 Cardio Protocol discussed in this book, or any fitness training program. Sprint 8 is anaerobic exercise, the most demanding form of exercise, and it has the most risks.

The purpose of this book is to educate, expand thinking about fitness as an informational source for readers, and it is not medical advice, nor has it been evaluated by the FDA. The publisher, author, and advisors shall have neither liability nor responsibility to any person or entity with respect to any loss or damage caused or alleged to be caused directly or indirectly by the information and programs contained in this book. If you do not agree with the above, you may return to the publisher for a full refund.

2016
Printed in USA by Pollock Printing, Nashville
Graphics by Manoj Bhargav *manojbhargavindia.blogspot.com*

Library of Congress Control Number: 2016903561
Cataloging-in-Publication
   Campbell, Phil
   Sprint 8 Cardio Protocol
   Includes bibliographical references and index.
ISBN: 9780692650028

   1. Physical fitness.   2. Exercise.   3. Health.
   4. Aging--Prevention. I. Title.

Contents

Part One *Ready*

Part Two *Set*

Part Three *GO!*

The impact of some of the deleterious effects of aging could be reduced if exercise focused on promoting Exercise-Induced Growth Hormone

- Dr. Richard Godfrey

Photo: Masters Track & Field 100 and 200 meter champion Nate Robertson running bleacher sprints with long-term training partner Phil Campbell

Foreword

Sprint 8 is the most revolutionary training tool to come along in decades. Phil Campbell has come up with the answer to the pressing issue of the poor physical condition of the average person today. What's more, Sprint 8 is also a tightly condensed routine, so that it fits into the busy person's harried time frame. That mix – a training routine that works and is short – is a winning combination. It is amazing to be able to get significant results from a program that lasts only 20 minutes in duration, but Phil has put such a program together with Sprint 8 and he has spent 40 years researching, testing and perfecting his cardio protocol.

Sprint 8 comes at the fitness arena from a totally different angle than other training programs. The Sprint 8 program enables whoever uses it to engage the key element that changes the body similar to injecting banned performance enhancing drugs, human growth hormone, *naturally*. Most workout routines come up short on this critical issue or miss it altogether but Sprint 8 successfully fires up human growth hormone in the body, creating significant positive change for people of all ages.

Sprint 8 is an entirely different approach than those that most programs employ. It gets people not to just work intensely, but it forces people to recruit both types of their *fast-twitch muscle cells,* an area many other programs ignore, and simply don't apply the science. The Sprint 8 Protocol has been carefully crafted over 40 years to recruit all three muscle fiber types thereby conditioning the anaerobic and aerobic processes of the heart muscle in many different ways that can be done by anyone at any age. Sprint 8 can be used for a lifetime. It's not the trend of the month or just another way to get the heart rate up to burn more calories.

Sprint 8 is no fad – it is a true athletic program that rapidly transforms the physique. And it will change the body for men and women, young and old. Sprint 8 is one of those rare programs that works for the long run – it will benefit you whenever and wherever you use it, and it keeps on working as long as you work it.

Another fantastic feature of Sprint 8 is its adaptability to any age group. Sprint 8 is viable for masters athletes and anyone who wants to get into top condition. Professional athlete to middle age to older adult can all benefit in this simple, time-efficient format. Twenty minutes, three times a week. That's all Phil is asking you to do.

If you are a teenager, the program will build you up. If you are 80, the same program will work for you too. The reason why is we all have three muscle fiber types that move the body and we have two processes of the heart muscle that we keep all of our lives.

With the Sprint 8 Protocol, Phil has taken the basis of his ground-breaking first book *Ready, Set, Go! Fitness* and adapted it to be used on various machines such as treadmills, recumbent bikes, elliptical machines and more. Virtually any cardio training tool you find in your gym can be used to perform Sprint 8.

Phil not only provides a superb training program, he also backs it up by showing how the latest research reveals the powerful effect Sprint 8 training has on the body. Past and current research shows that Sprint 8 is a very powerful transformational tool. Virtually all exercise benefits the body, but Phil has created the very best program, and a program that is exponentially better than the other options in the fitness world.

Sprint 8 should be the beginning point for any fitness consideration as it provides such a drastic, beneficial change to the body.

Sprint 8 is simple to understand and simple to put into play. If you honestly want to change your body, this is the best program to use. Sprint 8 provides the best possible way that 20 minutes of training can be used, and it provides the most reward for those 20 minutes. Its brief and intense training can transform the human physique in a short period of time like nothing else.

If you really want to improve your health with exercise. If you want to change your body right now, the Sprint 8 Cardio Protocol is the best choice you can make. - Dwayne Hines II

1

New Tools for a New You

This book is about giving you new tools to achieve a new you. A new you with more energy. A new you with improved cardiovascular fitness. A new you with less body fat, more muscle and stronger bones. A new you with enhanced optimism. And a new you with better health.

I almost forgot to mention that you can do all of this without starving. Yep, without starving. In fact, starving only sets you up to gain weight abnormally fast.

Does this sound too good to be true? It may sound like it. But I'm not asking you to blindly trust me. I'm going to prove it to you. This program works. And it will work for you.

The best news is a *New You* doesn't take nearly as long as you may think. But, you do need to trust this point. There are three parts in the book -- *READY*, *SET*, and *GO* sections. Before you start the *GO phase* -- the action phase where you apply principles in the book -- you should read, digest, and understand the first two sections, *READY* and *SET*. Then you will be prepared to implement the program, and most importantly, stick to it.

When new discoveries in science are correctly applied, you don't need two hours a day in a gym, and you don't have to starve to achieve your goals for a *New You*. We will look at the research together and see the best way to apply the science behind numerous new discoveries that will help you achieve your training goals.

New discoveries about your three *muscle-fiber types*. New discoveries about your body's three energy systems, and hormones released with a very specific form of short-duration cardio exercise will help guide the process. We will also see new discoveries about your cellular level mitochondria researchers call the nuclear power plants of the cells because this is where energy is made in the body to live life.

We will also look at new scientific discoveries about cellular level telomeres that are shown to protect your chromosomes and have promise in protecting the body from cancer and premature aging. All of these topics are related. And they tell us clearly and exactly how to exercise to get the best results possible from exercise, in the shortest amount of time.

I'm not going to waste your time throwing some out-of-context studies to make a point to try and impress you. My goal is simple. I will give you a reality based, doable, cardio program that will get you the best possible results in the shortest amount of time -- and without starving. If you can carve out 20 minutes, three-days-a-week, you are there. Four minutes of the 20 minutes is hard. It's the hardest four minutes of your life. But, 16 minutes of the 20 minutes is moving at the pace of a casual-paced walk.

All you have to do is two reps of 30 seconds followed by an easy and slow 90 seconds to get started. But please wait until you are armed with the information in the READY section and the SET section before you begin.

A NEW YOU!

To change your body, it's necessary to trim fat and build muscle. This is never an easy task, and it gets harder as we get older. Muscle mass naturally decreases and body fat increases as part of the aging process.

Fortunately you can slow down, stop, and even reverse this trend when you correctly apply new scientific discoveries about *muscle-fiber recruitment,* and select the best training tools to accomplish your goals.

When you select the correct tools, you will not only transform your body, you will also improve several critically important health measures during the process. Plus, you can accomplish this radical change in your body at any age, and you can do it in 20 minutes-a-day, three-days-per-week.

To improve health, it's necessary to strengthen both the aerobic and the anaerobic processes of your heart muscle. You'll learn how in this book.

To improve your appearance, you will learn how to drop body fat to look and feel better, but you will also learn how the cardio protocol in this book will release the hormone that has been shown to thicken skin by 7.1 percent.

Skin thickening doesn't mean much to us guys. But for middle age and older women, thickening your skin means that you are filling in the wrinkles, and estimated appearance benefit can be equal to looking as much as 20-years younger.

When we target these powerful hormones that are released in the body naturally with the right kind of exercise, great things can happen in many different areas.

The Body is Screaming at Us

The body is screaming at us through the research. It's trying to tell us exactly how to exercise for the best results. Sadly, we aren't listening. We are too hung up in following-the-follower and wandering from fad-to-fad that we miss the message behind the science. When we don't look at the real science behind claims, it's easy to miss the best the body has for us.

The end result of fitness-fad following is people get burned out and results come slower than expected., or they don't come at all. They get injured or get depressed and quit when the *after* photos look nothing like the ones they saw on TV.

Failure to lose body fat and see fitness improvement ultimately leads people to quitting. At this point people begin to suffer mentally and emotionally from the lack of energy because a well-meaning trainer said the reason you aren't getting results is because you didn't go on a drastic carbohydrate reduction diet or you need to stay in the target zone longer.

The great scapegoat of many failed exercise fad programs when they don't get results is, *well you didn't diet* (what they really mean is starve) *while doing the program*.

Clearly most people need to cut back on carbs and processed foods. A simple portion reduction goes a long way, but when someone applies the wrong set of tools based on flawed science, the end result can be disastrous. People begin thinking that all programs will fail unless they starve. And this is a huge mistake.

On the positive side, when you see the science and understand why the program in this book works, then you can put the little extra effort into the cardio reps and achieve all that the body can do for you. Today, the body is screaming at us, *when you exercise like this, the body will change and you can keep the changes without going on a starvation diet.*

Don't do this Protocol Unless . . .

It's vitally important that you understand the science behind the program to give you the motivation to continue. If you don't understand why you are doing this cardio protocol exactly as described, it will be very easy to jump to an another fitness fad, or go with an easier program, or even quit.

This program doesn't take a lot of time, but it's tough. It's tough in 30 seconds bite-size portions. Before you jump on your home exercise bike, or take off to the gym to try the protocol in this book, let's get you armed with some key principles that will help you achieve a new you in the quickest time possible without starving and without spending hours in the gym.

Your body adapts to the way you train

The number one principle in exercise science that every expert seems to agree with -- the body adapts. The body adapts positively to the way you train.

Adaptation to training simply means that if you want to run fast, you need to train fast. If an athlete, for example, trains heavy and slow, the body builds the slow-twitch muscle fiber and the slow muscle cells get stronger. The fast-muscle fibers don't get stronger because they don't get used.

One of the main reasons people fail to achieve their goals of reducing body fat and building muscle is that they take an old, slow approach based on science of *calories in and calories out* with hours of long / slow training. They don't purposely set out to take a drawn-out route. But they end up doing just that by following a conventional exercise program, which was typically created back-in-the-day when we thought muscle is a muscle, and before we knew about *muscle-fiber types* and how *muscle fiber* is activated during exercise. For example, many people begin jogging or some other slow and moderate-paced exercise to lose weight. This type of exercise program needs a near-starvation diet companion to see any results at all. And the results are short term, at best.

When the weight-loss process uses long and slow cardio for exercise, people typically become discouraged and quit after just a few months, and sometimes a few weeks. The research in this area is clear.

Losing weight with dieting *alone* means that you will gain it back. I'm sorry to tell you this, but people gain it back when they lose with diet alone. Losing weight with diet alone messes with your metabolism. Researchers report:

> *Caloric restriction results in fat loss; however, it may also result in loss of muscle and thereby reduce strength and aerobic capacity (VO2max). These effects may not occur with exercise-induced weight loss because of the anabolic effects of exercise on the heart and skeletal muscle... These findings suggest that during exercise-induced weight loss, the body adapts to maintain or even enhance physical performance capacity,*
> (Weiss, EP. (Nov 9, 2006) *Lower extremity muscle size and strength and aerobic capacity decrease with caloric restriction but not with exercise-induced weight loss* J Appl Physiol).

Research makes it clear. You can lose body fat when you diet, but you also lose muscle and this messes with your metabolism. Losing muscle makes it easier to gain the weight back when you leave the diet. This fat loss plan makes about as much sense as cutting off an arm to lose weight. Yeah, you'll weigh less, but it's really stupid. Losing weight with diet alone is the exact opposite of what someone should do.

If someone wants to lose weight, I typically advise, *add muscle and let the muscle eat away the fat permanently.* Taking this approach will help to keep the weight loss off. That is, as long as you continue to exercise and continue to eat a balanced diet in moderation, which generally involves some portion control.

A Better Approach

The Sprint 8 Protocol delivers better results in less time and with fewer workouts than you may expect. It is the exclusive, science-based protocol that uses the highest level of intensity for 30 seconds or less to achieve the best results. And it's important to know exactly why you get the best results from this type of short burst, super-high-intensity training.

Everyone can improve their results by adding intensity to their current method of exercise because that will typically raise your body temperature and increase calorie burning. But when you take it to the highest level of intensity, sprint intensity, this triggers a response in the body that melts fat and encourages muscle growth.

Sprint intensity is much more intense than interval training, and it's not easy. Sprint intensity isn't another form of interval training. Sprint intensity is in its own category. When very fit people who regularly do interval training try this sprint-intensity cardio protocol for the first time, I generally get a wide-eyed, near shock surprised look on their face with a comment like, *Wow, I had no idea there is such a difference.*

It's tough alright -- in 30 seconds or less bite-sized portions. But in many respects, it's the easiest program to stay with for a lifetime because it works. It works fast. And it only takes 20 minutes three-days-a-week.

This sprint-intensity protocol is incredibly efficient and produces near-unbelievable results. It also allows you to pack the most productive program into the least amount of time. The trick, of course, is doing it right.

The Sprint 8 Protocol is an optimized sprint-intensity cardio program that can be done on any type of cardio equipment as long as you can get totally winded in 30 seconds or less. How simple can it be. You can do Sprint 8 many different ways. The results will keep you coming back for more -- if you do it the right way.

When you follow the Sprint 8 Cardio Protocol exactly as described, you will see and physically feel noticeable improvements in a short amount of time. This approach is nothing short of radical for people of all ages.

The Sprint 8 Protocol forces positive muscle development and it burns fat quickly and effectively. It will help you achieve numerous desirable physical appearance changes. It will also improve several key health measures, *(Burt, D. (2012) Targeting exercise-induced growth hormone release: A novel approach to fighting obesity by substantially increasing endogenous GH serum levels naturally)*.

All Exercise Isn't Created Equal

The Sprint 8 Intensity Scale graphic shows how sprint-intensity cardio fits into the full range of exercise intensities. It's the toughest level. And it's much more intense than Interval training because pacing takes place in interval training. While interval training is more intense than steady-state cardio, it's significantly less intense than all-out, fast-fiber recruiting sprint-intensity cardio.

The good news is sprint-intensity only lasts 30 seconds OR LESS. It's simple; If you can go longer than 30 seconds, it's NOT sprint intensity.

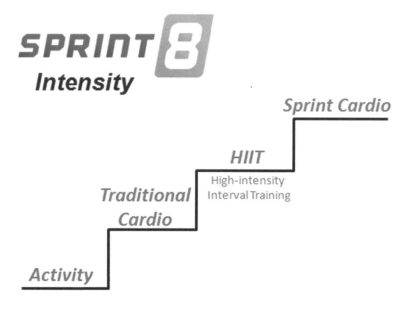

All exercise is beneficial for the body, but not all exercise has a significant impact on growth hormone release. This is why Sprint 8 was created years ago -- to target the maximum release of exercise-induced growth hormone and get all of the wonderful benefits this hormone produces, *naturally*.

In order to strongly stimulate a sizable growth hormone response, a workout has to be intense and meet the Sprint 8 benchmarks.

The flip side is that intense training, by its very nature, is very short. You get your workouts over with quickly and you also get to the reward -- more muscle, less fat, more quickly, (Savine, Sonksen. (2000) *Growth Hormone–hormone replacement for the somatopause*. Hormone Research. 53 Suppl 3:37-41).

Traditional exercise, such as going out for a jog or taking a long walk will burn calories. But this won't generate significant growth hormone production. Neither will pumping a few moderate dumbbells. That's why people who just rely on jogging or a similar activity often fall far short of reaching their full potential. The type of training required to trigger a significant release of growth hormone is a specific formula of high-intensity sprint cardio and a very specific 90-seconds active recovery in between each sprint-cardio repetition.

20 Minutes Gets it Done

As unlikely as it may seem, it is possible to realize significant benefits in a 20-minute workout. If you have 20 minutes, you can perform the Sprint 8 Protocol and spark the change in your body you want to see. And of the 20 minutes, only 4 minutes is all-out, fast-as-you-can-go, sprint-intensity work.

Hopefully, everyone should be able to carve out 20 minutes three-days-a-week -- especially if that something is improving your health, fighting the symptoms of aging, trimming fat and building a leaner body that has significantly more energy for life.

Researchers report on the efficiency and rapid improvement produced by sprint-intensity cardio:

> *A novel type of high-intensity interval training known as sprint interval training has demonstrated increases in aerobic and anaerobic performance with very low time commitment ... Our results suggest that intense interval training is indeed a time-efficient strategy to induce rapid metabolic and performance adaptations, (*Bayati M. (2011) *A practical model of low-volume high-intensity interval training induces performance and metabolic adaptations that resemble 'all-out' sprint interval training.* J Sports Sci Med. 2011 Sep 1;10(3):571-6.).

WHY IT WORKS

Unlike slow and moderate-intensity training, and even typical forms of interval training that have higher intensity intervals lasting longer than 30 seconds, all-out sprint-intensity cardio stimulates a huge natural release of growth hormone.

Please note that this isn't just a small release of this powerful hormone (so powerful that it determines how tall we become). It's a huge release -- so significant that if you were an Olympic athlete and your blood was drawn after doing Sprint 8, you would probably test false positive for injecting this banned substance. It's banned because it improves athletic performance.

While higher levels of exercise intensity offers many benefits, including a higher caloric burn rate, it is this natural stimulation of human growth hormone that is most beneficial. Elevated levels of human growth hormone are associated with increased lean muscle mass, decreased body fat and higher energy, (Godfrey, Madgwick, Whyte. (2003) *The exercise-induced growth hormone response in athletes.* Sports Medicine. 33(8):599-613).

The Sprint 8 Protocol is scientifically proven to stimulate the release of natural growth hormone by as much as 814 percent in hospital-based studies where growth hormone was measured before and immediately after doing Sprint 8. This level of increase in exercise-induced growth hormone triggers dramatic physical transformations in average, normal people and in the very fit population as well, (Burt, D. (2012)*Targeting exercise-induced growth hormone release: A novel approach to fighting obesity by substantially increasing endogenous GH serum levels naturally*).

When compared to pre-Sprint 8 baseline growth hormone levels for a study group, the increase of the powerful hormone was astonishing. One hospital-based study indicated an 814% average increase in growth-hormone levels from a pre-Sprint 8 baseline blood-draw lab test to post-Sprint 8 lab test.

To understand the significance of this huge release of growth hormone, produced by the cardio protocol in this book, it's important for you to know how powerful this hormone is in the human body.

Growth hormone is produced by the pituitary gland, which is called the master gland because of its importance. This is the same hormone that makes us grow taller.

Just think about this for a moment. Think about how powerful this substance is in the body. It determines how tall we become. Once we reach our full height, the hormone is the same substance, but it changes roles.

Distinguished researcher, Dr. Thomas Welbourne says it should be called your *fitness hormone.*

Dr. Richard Godfrey says, *The impact of some of the negative effects of aging could be reduced if exercise focused on promoting exercise produced growth hormone.* Dr. Godfrey also uses Sprint 8 in his personal training. He writes,

> *I have been using the Sprint 8 Workout three times a week (usually on an exercise bike but sometimes running) and I have lost about 7 pounds in weight. I have noticed my recovery after almost every activity (even walking up two flights of stairs) has improved dramatically.*
> - Dr. Richard Godfrey

The exciting news is that you don't have to inject this hormone to receive its benefits. The Sprint 8 Protocol can be your personal tool to give yourself this huge NATURAL injection of this very powerful hormone with a 20 minute, three-day-a-week workout.

Growth hormone does many important health related things in the body. It helps to regulate body composition, muscle and bone growth, sugar and fat metabolism, and it's shown to possibly have an important role in heart function. The body releases growth hormone when you are in deep sleep and the body releases a significant amount of this powerful hormone during Sprint 8. Researchers report:

Growth hormone (GH) regulates whole body metabolism, and physical exercise is the most potent stimulus to induce its secretion in humans, (Ignacio D. (2015, Apr 13) *Thyroid hormone and estrogen regulate exercise-induced growth hormone release).*

In practical terms, this means after 8 weeks of Sprint 8, three-times-per-week, the study participants had significantly changed their body composition. They reduced their *body fat* by 27 percent and lowered their *bad LDL cholesterol* and *triglycerides* significantly while increasing the *good HDL cholesterol,* (Burt, D. (2012) *Targeting exercise-induced growth hormone release)*.

In a related study, researchers reported;

> ***Sprint interval training led to a significant increase in lactate and the anabolic factors growth hormone, insulin-like growth factor, IGF binding protein, and testosterone levels.*** (Meckel, Y. (2011) *Hormonal and inflammatory responses to different types of sprint interval training,* J Strength Cond Res. 2011 Aug;25(8):2161-9).

Professor Steve Boutcher, a University of New South Wales researcher states this type of high-intensity training is much better for weight loss than other forms of exercise. He reports:

> ***Most exercise protocols designed to induce fat loss have focused on regular steady state exercise at a moderate intensity. Disappointingly, these kinds of protocols have led to negligible weight loss.*** *However, other forms of exercise may have a greater impact on body composition. For example,* ***emerging research examining high-intensity intermittent exercise (HIIE) indicates that it may be more effective at reducing subcutaneous and abdominal body fat than other types of exercise.*** (Boutcher, S.H. (2011) *High-Intensity Intermittent Exercise and Fat.* J Obes. 2011; 868305. PMCID: PMC2991639).

Sprint Intensity

Sprint intensity is the secret to the clinical successes of the Sprint 8 Protocol. Sprint-intensity exercise is not easy, but it is the factor that yields the best results in the shortest time. The human body is amazing. It has the ability to respond to the challenges it faces. If someone lies around all day on the sofa watching television, the body adapts to the way it's trained (or not trained in this case) and the body turns into a puffy couch potato.

Likewise, if you train like a sprinter with the Sprint 8 Protocol, your body adapts to training by becoming more like a sprinter's body. The body has an incredible ability to morph into a new shape in order to respond to whatever it is faced with. And sprint-intensity training can bring an intense change in the body's composition.

When using Sprint 8 as a tool, you are forcing the body to recruit and build all three *muscle fiber type*s and release exercise-induced growth hormone. This causes the body to adapt and change to handle the new stimulus -- and this process makes the body stronger, leaner, and healthier.

Sprint-intensity training is the secret that makes it possible to slow down the typical symptoms of aging while most people choose to accelerate the symptoms of aging with poor lifestyle choices.

Everyone knows they need to exercise regularly. Time barriers and family responsibility is what trips up most people. Sprint 8 is a weapon for time-crunched adults. It allows you to pack a huge amount of training productivity into a very short time frame. This is so important that it needs to be repeated - sprint-intensity training yields high productivity results in the shortest time frame. Sprint 8 is the perfect solution for today's busy culture. The Sprint 8 Protocol provides the ability to get and stay super fit even if you have a hectic schedule. Researchers report:

> *Sprint Interval Training (SIT) improves aerobic capacity in healthy, young people. Relative to continuous endurance training of moderate intensity, SIT presents an equally **effective alternative with a reduced volume of activity,*** (Gist N. (2014 Feb), *Sprint interval training effects on aerobic capacity: a systematic review and meta-analysis.* Sports Med. 44(2):269-79).

Growth Hormone Benefits

Growth hormone has a tremendously beneficial effect on the human physique. Growth hormone effectively fights the symptoms of aging, obesity, weight gain, and less than desirable energy levels, but it also increases lean muscle. Elevated levels of growth hormone are associated with increased lean mass, muscle tone, decreased body fat, fewer wrinkles and higher energy.

Studies show growth hormone can boost lean mass by 8.8 percent while lowering body fat by 14.4 percent. Growth hormone is not only the hormone that determines how tall we grow, it is able to create a dramatic change in the body that causes muscle to grow and fat to melt at the same time, (Rudman, New England Journal of Medicine, 1990).

Growth hormone is such a powerful substance. It can make many positive changes in the body. When you are able to get growth hormone circulating with an exercise-induced release in your system, good things begin to happen to your physique, (Pritzlaff (1990 Aug). *Impact of acute exercise intensity on pulsatile growth hormone release in men.* Journal of Applied Physiology. 1990 Aug;87(2):498-504).

When comparing the impact of exercise-induced growth hormone from the Sprint 8 Protocol in an eight-week study, a group of test subjects weighing on average 194 pounds experienced a drop in body fat of 22.39 pounds while gaining 13.39 pounds of lean mass. That's a significant gain in lean mass while cutting body fat at the same time.

Their average weight went from 194 to 185 pounds in eight weeks of Sprint 8, three-times-a-week and without changing diet (diet would not be a variable in the study). The average body-fat loss in this group classified as the *General Population Group* (of those wanting to improve health, reduce body fat, and lose more than 10 pounds) clearly shows they achieved their goals. The average drop in body fat was 27.8 percent. One of the physicians on the panel said *the only way you get more body fat off than this, is to cut it off.* Sprint 8 takes you out of a calorie counting world when it comes to results and places you in a world of injecting hormones at an anti-aging center, except, Sprint 8 is all natural.

Step out of a Calorie-Counting World

A reduction in body fat of 27.8 percent in two studies, in eight weeks time, without dieting, is near unbelievable. I know it is, but I continually hear and see these results repeated. The results come from 20 minutes, three-times-a-week, sprint-intensity cardio performed the right way.

When looking at the results of the Sprint 8 Protocol, it's more like comparing results from injecting powerful hormones and steroids than comparing to traditional long / slow cardio exercise.

In fact, when the Sprint 8 studies were designed, they were based on the premise that Sprint 8 will mimic the results of injecting growth hormone, which gets an average reduction in body fat of 14.4 percent. When the results of both hospital-based studies came back with an average drop in body fat of *27 percent,* I was shocked. This means that the exercise method, the totally natural method (Sprint 8, three-times-a-week for eight weeks), is almost twice as effective in reducing body fat as injecting growth hormone daily.

Melissa Waters, a Nutrition Coach with a BS degree in Dietetics with emphasis in Holistic Health from San Francisco State University, analyzed the research data. She reported when comparing the body-fat-reducing results of Sprint 8 with burning calories from exercise, ***you can do Sprint 8, 20 minutes three-times-a-week or get the same results by doing cardio three-hours-a-day for SEVEN-days-a-week at 75% intensity***.

This is a 21 to 1 ratio when comparing the impact exercise-induced growth hormone gets via Sprint 8 three-days-a-week for 20 minutes (1 hour a week) versus 21 hours of cardio at 75 percent intensity. And 75 percent intensity cardio isn't a walk in the park.

Sprint 8 is a no-brainer for healthy people in the general population. Not only does Sprint 8 get superior results for the *General Population Group,* it gets great results for those who are very fit. Eight weeks of Sprint 8 in a group of fit people (*Fit Group*) who wanted to improve health, trim body fat without dieting, and weight loss wasn't a priority, also achieved their goals.

The *Fit Group* gained 1.28 pounds of lean mass, and they reduced their body fat by 13.9 percent without changing their diets The *Fit Group* started with an average body weight of 169.18 pounds and ended at 163.26 pounds for an average weight loss of 6.42 pounds.

The *Fit Group* burned a calculated ratio of 10 to 1. This means if you are in *Fit Group* category, **one hour of Sprint 8 per week** (20 minutes, three per week) **will reduce body fat equal to the calorie burning of doing 3.5 hours of cardio at 75 percent intensity** three-days-a-week.

If I asked you to take your choice of 20 minutes -- of which 4 minutes is sprint-intensity cardio and 16 minutes is casual-paced recovery, OR you can do 75 percent intensity cardio for 3.5 hours on those same three days, my hunch is most people would choose 20 minutes, three-days-a-week.

If you are in the *General Population* who want to lose more than 10 pounds, drop body fat, and improve health, there is no real choice. It's Sprint 8, 20 minutes three-days-a-week, OR three-hours-a-day at 75 percent intensity for seven days.

Here's how to apply this formula, if you are in the *Fit Group*, take what ever number you see on the calorie-burning meter on your cardio unit during Sprint 8, multiply it by 10 to estimate the impact of exercise-induced growth hormone has on your body in body fat loss. If you are in the *General Population Group*, multiply the calorie number by 20 -- that is -- if you are doing the Sprint 8 the right way.

Building Muscle Raises Resting Metabolism

Training with intensity creates micro-fiber tears in the muscles propelling the exercise. This starts the process that builds muscle. Whether it's sprint cardio or strength training, creating micro-fiber tears raises resting metabolism -- so when you are just sitting there, your muscles require more energy to heal and recover.

Distinguished researcher, Dr. Wayne Westcott describes this process:

> *At rest, every pound of untrained muscle uses between 5 and 6 calories per day for protein breakdown and synthesis. However, every pound of resistance-trained muscle uses approximately 9 calories per day for more extensive protein breakdown and repair processes. Resistance exercise produces tissue microtrauma that requires relatively large energy supplies for muscle remodeling. Research reveals that a single strength training session can increase resting energy expenditure by 5 percent to 9 percent for three days after the workout,* (Westcott, W. (July/Aug 2015), *Build Muscle, Improve Health: Benefits Associated with Resistance Exercise,* Vol. 19/No.4. ACSMs Health & fitness Journal. p.23).

If you're a female, I'm not talking about building *linebacker neck* kind of muscles. First of all, this can't happen unless you inject *male* hormones.

What I'm talking about is adding a little muscle throughout your entire body. This will actually make most women appear leaner, more fit, and healthier. Building muscle has huge benefits for everyone at all ages, but it's especially important for women.

Sprint 8 will provide women with a time-efficient tool to build muscle. Releasing growth hormone itself will be helpful, but Sprint 8 forces you to recruit all three *muscle fiber types* to propel the exercise, whereas most forms of cardio exercise only recruit the *slow-muscle fiber*. Interval training typically only recruits the *fast-IIa muscle fiber* and, while hard, it generally doesn't recruit the *super-fast IIx muscle fiber* that lays dormant and tries not to be used unless you need to run away from a bad guy.

Sprint 8 forces you to recruit, develop and strengthen more muscle fiber than any other form of exercise. And it saves you time. Sprint 8 will save you a lot of time. And you will get better results. With Sprint 8, if you do it right, more is less. You never need to do more than 8 reps, and you never need to spend more than 20 minutes, three-days-a-week for the sprint cardio part of training.

Get Your Growth Hormone Naturally Not from a Needle

I think almost everyone will agree that the best way to get the benefits of growth hormone is naturally. In 30 years of promoting Sprint 8, the only people who seem to disagree with the natural method of getting the benefits of growth hormone are those selling injections or supplements claiming to increase growth hormone.

Every year there's some company claiming to have an exercise pill. If you will look closely at their claim, you will probably see that they are trying to increase this hormone with a pill. Research shows 2 grams of inexpensive L-glutamine has a positive impact on growth hormone release.

I recommend experimenting with L-glutamine (2 grams or 2000 mg) 30 minutes to an hour before training. There is mainstream research to back this up. But I don't sell supplements and I don't advertise supplement brands.

Almost everyone will agree when the natural path is taken, the results are the healthiest for the body. When you utilize the natural method for increasing growth hormone, the body works *with*, instead of against itself.

Many athletes and healthy people interested in building the body and looking younger have caught on to the idea of the benefits of growth hormone. Unfortunately, many have gone about increasing their growth hormone levels the wrong way. Rather than using the right kind of sprint-intensity exercise, sleep and mainstream nutrition, they have resorted to injecting synthetic growth hormone to get the benefits.

Granted, there aren't tons of studies showing that injecting growth hormone is bad. But it doesn't take rocket science to figure out when people inject a man-made substance into the body every day to achieve quick and easy results, you know there is a long term health price to pay. There always is for taking unwise short cuts.

Synthetic human growth hormone (HGH) in healthy adults can cause side effects and hazards for the body. *Web MD* cites possible side effects:

> *Nerve, muscle, or joint pain*
> *Carpal tunnel syndrome*
> *Numbness and tingling of the skin*
> *High cholesterol levels*
> *Increased risk of diabetes*
> *Increased risk contributing to the growth of cancerous tumors*

Wow, did you notice the last one. The *growth of cancerous tumors* is the big unknown that physician friends fear the most. While some physicians will argue there isn't a body of research to prove this, other physicians make the point, *why take the chance with the unknown*, you are gambling with your health, (Dunkin, Ratini, *Human Growth Hormone*, Dec 30, 2014, http://www.webmd.com/fitness-exercise/human-growth-hormone-hgh?page=2).

Mary Anne Dunkin, in an article on human growth hormone reports in *HGH Uses and Abuses* for *Wed MD* concerning children and adults:

> *Synthetic human growth hormone was developed in 1985 and approved by the FDA for specific uses in children and adults.*
>
> *In children, HGH injections are approved for treating short stature of unknown cause as well as poor growth due to a number of medical causes, including:*
> **Turner's syndrome, genetic disorder affecting a girl's development*
> **Prader-Willi syndrome, an uncommon genetic disorder causing poor muscle tone, low levels of sex hormones, and a constant feeling of hunger*
> **Chronic kidney insufficiency*
> **Children born small for gestational age*
>
> *In adults, approved uses of HGH include:*
> **Short bowel syndrome, a condition in which nutrients are not properly absorbed due to severe intestinal disease or the surgical removal of a large portion of the small intestine*
> **HGH deficiency due to rare pituitary tumors or their treatment*
> **Muscle-wasting disease associated with HIV/AIDS*
>
> *But the most common uses for HGH are **not** FDA-approved. Some people use the hormone, along with other performance-enhancing drugs such as anabolic steroids in an attempt to build muscle and improve athletic performance...*
> *The use of HGH for anti-aging is **not** FDA-approved,* (Dunkin, Ratini, *Human Growth Hormone (HGH)*, Dec 30, 2014, http://www.webmd.com/fitness-exercise/human-growth-hormone-hgh)

It is much wiser to work with your body instead of against it. This means stimulating your body's own growth hormone instead of injecting it with an outside (synthetic) source. If you are thinking about injecting growth hormone, maybe you should consider doing the eight week Sprint 8 Challenge first.

Do the Sprint 8 Cardio Protocol for eight weeks and monitor your body fat, muscle composition and your cholesterol *before* and *after* the eight weeks.

You might also ask your physician why he or she doesn't recommend trying the natural method to increase growth hormone first. Now, if your physician gave you this book or my first book, *Ready, Set, GO! Fitness*, (as many physicians do) before sending you to an anti-aging specialist, thank your physician for truly caring about your health by giving you options.

Turning on your growth hormone release process naturally with sprint-intensity cardio can significantly change your body for the better. You get all of the upsides of human growth hormone stimulation without risking the side effects synthetic hormones can cause.

Training with an Edge

Achieving the highest level of intensity for 30 seconds or less holds the keys to the kingdom. It provides the training edge that transforms the body to its potential, and it does it in much less time than other models of training. However, the highest level of intensity needs to be applied in a very specific manner to maximize the potential of the human body.

High-intensity training in general will help build the body, but when you apply sprint-intensity in a specific manner, the results are near-unbelievable. Researchers show the results can actually mimic taking injections of growth hormone that typically reduces body fat by 14.4 percent and increases lean mass by 8.8 percent. Researchers report:

> *Our findings suggest that exercise training is a feasible intervention in GH-deficient adults. The beneficial effects of exercise can mimic the effects of GH treatment,* (Thomas SG, *Exercise training benefits growth hormone-deficient adults in the absence or presence of GH treatment.* J Clin Endocrinol Metab. 2003 Dec;88(12):5734-8).

Researchers show when intensity is tailored to a specific training mode it provides incredible results. This is what Sprint 8 is all about -- applying the science of muscle recruitment (of all *three muscle-fiber types* and three energy systems), conditioning not only the aerobic process of the heart muscle but also the anaerobic process, and making the protocol realistic for every person at all ages so everyone can achieve the most impressive results possible in the shortest time.

The Sprint 8 Protocol provides the best possible way to apply sprint-intensity cardio because it works both processes of your heart muscle -- the aerobic and the anaerobic processes. Sprint 8 provides a comprehensive exercise to recruit and work all three muscle fiber types.

The Sprint 8 Protocol is realistic. It only takes 20 minutes, three-days-a-week. Sprint 8 provides near unlimited variety. It can be done in numerous different ways. It can be done on any piece of cardio equipment that you would find in a commercial fitness center. As long as you can get totally winded in 30-seconds or less on the cardio unit, you can do Sprint 8.

The Sprint 8 Cardio Protocol is programmed in Matrix Fitness commercial cardio units made by Johnson Health Tech, and it's programmed in Vision Fitness light-commercial and home cardio units.

In revolutionary research published by the *National Institutes of Health*, Dr. Richard Godfrey, a distinguished researcher at Brunel University in London introduces an entirely new approach that departs from the *calories burned* typical way of thinking about exercise productivity.

Dr. Godfrey is a Senior Lecturer in Sports Coaching and Human Performance. His research is in the area of human growth hormone and specifically the exercise-induced growth hormone response to exercise. Dr. Godfrey concludes:

> *The impact of some of the negative effects of aging could be reduced **if exercise focused on promoting exercise produced growth hormone**, (Godfrey. R. The exercise-induced growth hormone response in athletes. Sports Med. 2003;33(8):599-613).*

Dr. Godfrey is an expert in exercise-induced growth hormone and he does the Sprint 8. He commented, *I have also been able to use the **energy boost** this type of training has given me to get back into some 'proper' sports training.* Please take note of Dr. Godfrey's comment about the Sprint 8 induced energy boost. We will come back to this in the chapter *Need More Energy.*

High-Intensity + Right Formula = Success

The process of stimulating growth hormone is simple, yet not easy. The discomfort lies in the fact that the cardio protocol has to achieve four benchmarks to produce a significant release of growth hormone. It doesn't just take high-intensity cardio. It takes maximum-intensity, all-out for 30-seconds, sprint-intensity cardio to release this huge amount of growth hormone.

Maximum intensity can be very uncomfortable. Sprint-intensity training, by its very nature, is brief. True sprint-intensity cardio is so intense that it can only be sustained for 30 seconds or less. In fact, if you can go longer than 30 seconds, this means you held back and you paced. And pacing is the enemy of intensity. If you can do a cardio sprint for longer than 30 seconds, don't count the rep.

Training at an all-out, sprint-intensity level requires maximum physical and mental involvement. It requires pushing the body hard, as hard as you can. It's tough, but the upside is huge. You get your workouts over quickly, and you achieve the benefits faster (less body fat, more muscle, thicker skin, thicker bones, and a lot more energy for life). And it doesn't take an hour in the gym every day. In our busy society, this is a huge plus factor.

There are actually three levels of intensity for the discussions in this book. *Low* and *Moderate* intensity are in group one.

Moving up on the intensity scale is group two, *High Intensity* that is frequently called *HIT*, *HIIT*, *Boot Camp* training, or *HIIE* (high-intensity intermittent exercise).

The highest level is *Maximum Intensity,* or more aptly called *Sprint Intensity* in this book. The Sprint 8 Cardio Protocol clearly falls into the Maximum Intensity category on the following chart.

Cardio Intensity Training Levels

Low & Moderate Intensity Training
Traditional Slow Cardio
Propelled by Type I slow-muscle fiber
Aerobic process of heart muscle conditioned
Metabolic energy system conditioned;
Aerobic Benefits: traditional calorie burning
Results are dependent on very long duration & strict dieting

High-Intensity Training
Interval training, HIT, HIIT, Boot Camp training
Propelled by slow Type I & some Type II fast-muscle fiber
Aerobic process of heart muscle conditioned
   with some anaerobic process
Metabolic energy system conditioned; Lactate (Glycolysis System)
Benefits: enhanced calorie burning due to increased body
temperature
Results: Significantly better results than traditional slow cardio,
   multi tasks strength training opportunities with cardio

Sprint-Intensity Training
Sprint 8 Cardio Protocol
Propelled by all three muscle fiber types;
   Slow, Type IIa fast-muscle fiber & IIx super-fast muscle fiber
Anaerobic & aerobic processes of heart muscle conditioned
All three metabolic energy systems conditioned;
   ATP-CP (Phosphagen System)
Results: Mimic taking growth hormone injections
   Step out of a calorie counting world into a hormone
   injecting world except it's totally NATURAL

How quick does it take to start seeing benefits of sprint-intensity training? As amazing as it may seem, it is possible to feel and see the benefits from the Sprint 8 Cardio Protocol during the first couple of workouts.

Sprint Intensity Performed Safely

Movement is an indicator of your physical condition. The speed of movement when you exercise is critical. The faster you can move, the more likely you are to be in good condition. Conversely, always moving slowly is an indicator things are starting to fall apart. Movement is vital to keeping the human body working well. Fast movement is at the top of the movement hierarchy. Movement -- particularly the ability to move quickly -- shows life, vitality and fitness level.

An important goal of this book is to give you tools. The main one being a time-efficient, effective, cardio protocol, and also the motivation for you to safely add sprint-cardio exercise to your lifestyle. Not just for an eight-week test drive (which is a great way to start), but my goal is for you to continue this 20 minute, three-day-a-week program safely for a life time -- a life time where you enjoy supreme health, fitness and revved up energy for an exciting life, all-of-your-life. Sprint 8 is hard. There's nothing harder. It will do what I'm saying it will do. But it's important to start the sprint-intensity cardio journey knowing there is a progressive building going on in your body.

It's always a good idea to have your physician clear you for anaerobic exercise before starting sprint cardio, or any new exercise program -- especially if you have been sedentary. The goal is to strengthen your heart muscle, not harm it. If someone has clogged arteries, does high-intensity exercise, and the blood can't flow, it can significantly damage the heart muscle.

It's also a great idea to get a cholesterol test before beginning the Sprint 8 Protocol so you can track your success with basic health measurements. Seeing your physician and obtaining a cholesterol test *before* and *after* eight weeks of Sprint 8, will help provide additional motivation to stay-the-course and continue.

You will be using muscle fiber that may not have been recruited and worked in a few years. You will be using muscles, tendons, ligaments and joints at higher speeds -- perhaps higher than they have ever moved before. The foundation for sprint-cardio intensity needs to develop and build safely. It's important to not jump-the-gun and false start with a pulled hamstring by going to the track and sprint running 8 reps of 60-meter sprints before you finish this chapter. Please finish reading the book and get *Ready* and *Set*, **before** jumping to the GO implementation phase.

Step one for every possible method of doing the Sprint 8 is the *warm up.* This applies to all ages. *Warm up* is necessary to do the Sprint 8 Protocol safely. Athlete, fitness club member, professional athlete all need to *warm up* before doing Sprint 8.

Rather than heading to the track, going to the fitness club to start the Sprint 8 Protocol on one of these cardio units will provide some protection for the hamstrings and calves that aren't high-velocity, *fast-muscle fiber* conditioned (at least not yet). Learning the Sprint 8 on a recumbent cycle or elliptical unit is the best way to begin Sprint 8.

You can run the Sprint 8 on a track, but this requires a progressive, lengthy, fast-fiber building program to safely handle the intensity of sprint running. The *fast-muscle fiber* foundation can take several weeks (and even months) before the hamstrings are ready to run sprints full speed.

Sprint running means you are carrying your full-body weight and throwing it violently forward 5 to 6 feet with every foot strike using the strength of your hamstrings, glutes, calf muscles, and achilles -- one leg at a time.

Sprint running on a treadmill is safer on the hamstrings than sprint running on a track because you are *toeing up* while the treadmill belt moves under you. Sprint running on a track means you are throwing your body several feet *forward* -- not just *up* -- but *up* and *forward.* This is too intense on the hamstrings until the foundation is constructed. The details of running Sprint 8 on a track will be discussed in Chapter 8, *The Sprint 8 Cardio Protocol.*

Sprint 8 on a cardio unit means three minutes of *warm up* on the specific cardio machine you'll be doing Sprint 8 on -- you are *warming* the precise muscles, tendons and ligaments that will be used during the cardio sprint.

Start out at a low resistance level, generally level 1 or 2 on most cardio machines, for the *warm up.* After three minutes of *warm up,* your body should be ready to go.

Each cardio sprint is all about moving as fast you can for 30 seconds or less, but the point here is that sprint-intensity can be performed safely, especially on a cardio machine.

Researchers report the effectiveness of a 30-second cardio sprint:

> *The study results agree with the **effectiveness of a 30 second all-out training program** with a reduced time commitment for anthropometric, aerobic and anaerobic adaptation **and eliminate doubts about its safety as a model**,* (Nalcakan GR. *The Effects of Sprint Interval vs. Continuous Endurance Training on Physiological And Metabolic Adaptations in Young Healthy Adults.* J Hum Kinet. 2014 Dec 30;44:97-109).

Interval training, which is similar but *less* intense than sprint cardio, is shown to be positive for people who are overweight. They report: ***This format of exercise was found to be well tolerated in an overweight population***, *(Sim, AJ. High-intensity intermittent exercise attenuates ad-libltum energy intake.* Int J Obes (Lond). 2014 Mar;38(3):417-22).

The researchers in this study also learned this type of training suppresses the hormone that makes us hungry, *ghrelin*. In another study, researchers show that *stem cells* are increased in muscles with elevated growth hormone:

> *Growth hormone may play an additional role in skeletal muscle by regulation of stem cells, as **increased stem cell numbers are found in human muscle with increased growth hormone levels,*** (Heinemeier, KM. (2012, Mar 1). *GH/IGF-I axis and matrix adaptation of the musculotendinous tissue to exercise in humans.* Sc and J Med Sci Sports).

Seemingly every month, there are new studies showing numerous positive benefits of sprint-intensity 8 cardio benefits. This is far different than 30-years ago when I began using sprint-intensity cardio to improve health, fitness and manage weight and cholesterol.

The Sprint 8 Cardio Protocol has worked well for many people over the last 30 years, and it can work for you.

Muscles are the engines of our bodies.
Muscles are where combustion occurs,
where energy is released, where power is
produced, and where movement originates.

- Dr. Wayne Westcott

(*ACSM's Health & Fitness Journal,* July/Aug 2015 p.22)

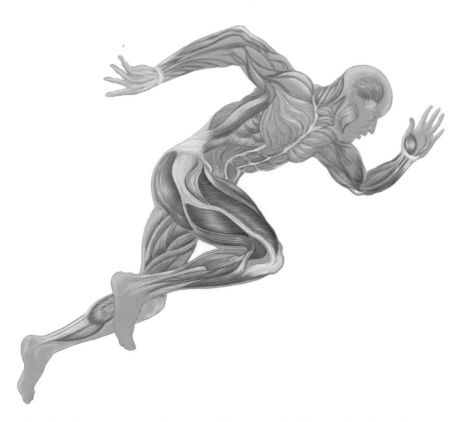

The body adapts to the way it's trained. It's pretty simple.
Train like a sprinter, look like a sprinter.

2

Train like a Sprinter Look like a Sprinter

Ever wonder why sprinters look the way they do? Sprinters typically have lots of muscle and very little body fat. Think about how athletes in sprinting sports look. Sprinting sports like football, soccer, baseball, softball, lacrosse, field hockey, and rugby are sprinting sports. Basketball has brief moments of sprinting. Think about how all these athletes look. They have lots of muscle and very little body fat.

The body adapts to the way it's trained. Strength training heavy and slow makes people strong and slow. Training for a sprinting sport trains all three muscle fiber types and achieves the benchmarks necessary to release huge amounts of exercise-induced growth hormone.

You can do the same thing the sprinting athlete can do if you do sprint-intensity cardio. You are, in many respects, just like all of these sprinting athletes. These athletes have *three muscle fiber types.* You have *three muscle fiber types.* But because we don't use the *fast-muscle fiber* in fitness training, those muscle cells (that can be as much as half of your muscle cells), are small **because they don't get recruited and used during exercise**. But when they do, this is when you can achieve your potential.

Amazing Human Performance Potential

Comparing the peak performance of aging track & field sprinters shows what the potential is for all human beings as they age (if they use sprint-intensity cardio in their fitness training). The results are quite amazing.

From the viewpoint of speed and peak performance, the graphic shows for every five years of life, peak performance goes down. But this is extremely positive because it only goes down *a little*.

To see human potential, look at the following graphic and compare age group World Records (in tenths) with the current 100-meter track World Record.

Age Group 100m World Records Compared to Current World Record

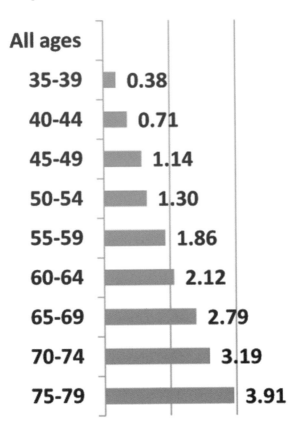

While the Olympic Sprint Team wouldn't be a realistic goal for middle age adults and older, outstanding results in body-fat loss, muscle building and fitness improvement can still be achieved with sprint-intensity cardio at any age.

Look at the graphic and compare the 60-65 year old masters sprinter in terms of fitness and performance with the best of the best in different age groups. The chart shows the 60-year old masters World Record holder is only 1.78 tenths-of-a-second behind the finish line of his 35 year-old counterpart.

Now think about this. At age 60, this man is only 2.12 tenths-of-a-second slower than the current world record holder Usain Bolt, who ran 100 meters in 9.58 seconds in his early 20s. Think about the profound significance to his potential and performance. Visualize Usain Bolt finishing the race, then count *one-thousand one, one-thousand two,* and boom, the 60-year old man sprints across the finish line.

Even better, Usain Bolt crosses the finish line, then count *one-thousand one, one-thousand two* and before you can finish *one-thousand three,* a 65-year old sprints past the finish line.

Compare this 60-year old and 65-year old to most men their ages. Many in their 60's have trouble casual-pace walking and are primary targets of companies selling a death trap -- a motorized wheelchair type machine that will further erode their muscle and bone density. Don't walk away from these machines. Don't run away from these machines. Sprint away! Instead, buy a cardio machine with Sprint 8 that's made for Sprint 8 intensity.

These age group world records clearly show us the potential we have for fitness and performance during aging. Let me say this one more time. These age group world records clearly show us the potential we have for fitness and performance during aging.

None of these masters sprinters will make the Olympic Team, but just think of the human potential, or better, think of the potential *YOU* have if you add sprint-intensity cardio to your training plan and keep it for a lifetime.

At age 75, when many are headed to the nursing home, this graph clearly makes the case for the human potential to be at such a level of health and fitness that a 75-year old is only 3.91 tenths-of-a-second behind the 100-meter world record. Think about that.

At age 75, I'll take that deal all day long!

Case Study, Dr. Derick Phan

While most athletes see their performance times slightly slow down every year, 42-year old, Dr. Derick Phan used Sprint 8 training to improve his performance. Dr. Phan is an Orthodontist in San Jose, California. He does the Sprint 8 Challenge Class 7 a.m. Monday, Wednesday, and Friday mornings.

Dr. Phan began running the 60-meter sprint in masters track & field events in a time of 8.31 seconds. He ran a 60-meter sprint (*below, second to left*) in Budapest, Hungary in 7.99 seconds. He did a two-session Speed Technique class with me that focuses on perfect speed mechanics during sprinting, and he joined the Sprint 8 Challenge class.

At age 42, his time is less than two tenths behind the World Record 6.39 set by Maurice Green in 1998.

Visualize this to see true human potential. Maurice Green crosses the finish line to break the World Record, then count *one-thousand one*, and before you get to *one-thousand two*, the 42-year old orthodontist is there. This is healthy aging.

Dr. Phan's performance continues to improve. In six months, his performance improved from a 8.31 60-meter sprint to 7.99, 7.96 and 7.68, which reverses the trend of aging sprinters slowing down. Obviously, sprinters will slow-down slightly as they age, but Dr. Phan shows us the power of working *fast-muscle fiber* and tapping in to all the body has to offer with exercise-induced growth hormone.

Dr. Phan says, *Sprint 8 has helped me transform from a 42-year old orthodontist to a Masters All American sprinter in just a few short months.*

While weight loss wasn't a primary goal for Dr. Phan (like it is for most people), he is one of the *Fit Group* discussed on page 20, *Step out of a Calorie-Counting World.*

During the eight week Sprint 8 Challenge, he gained 2.4 pounds of muscle and dropped 3.7 pounds of body fat, which is a 12 percent reduction in body fat. The case study with Dr. Phan demonstrates Sprint 8 can improve physical performance, and (even in a very fit population) significantly improve body composition by building muscle and reducing body fat.

Sprint Cardio Perfect for Women

What about sprint training for women? At this point, I was going to compare the age 40 group and show how they should be slowing down, but Gail Devers shows human potential even better. Gail Devers – at AGE 40 -- must have missed the class about slowing down during aging.

Gail Devers at age 40 was too busy winning sprinting events at major track meets to slow down. She had been on Olympic teams as a hurdler and 100-meter sprinter for years. After taking 19 months off to have a baby, she came back and not only competed, she won. In February 2007, 40-year old Gail Devers lined up at the starting blocks and finished first place in a major indoor track meet by beating all the young, college-age athletes in the US in the 60-meter hurdles.

How is it that a 40-year old woman can line-up side-by-side with the fastest athletes in the US and even think she has a chance to compete, much less win? Here's the secret. Gail Devers has maintained her *fast-twitch* muscle fiber by performing sprint-intensity training throughout the years. And with new research, we know the body itself produces the most powerful body-fat cutting, muscle-toning substance known in science naturally with sprint-intensity cardio, growth hormone.

Is sprint cardio a man's thing? Heck no! Listen ladies. You can do Sprint 8. Male or female, most people never live up to their human performance and fitness potential because they use the wrong tools.

They are trying to burn calories at magazine-paced, *slow-muscle fiber* propelled cardio that only works the heart muscle aerobically with an occasional starvation diet along the way to keep the weight off. When starving doesn't work, many people develop a defeated attitude that keeps them from trying.

We need to give people a realistic exercise tool to get the job done within a hectic, extremely busy lifestyle because everyone is busy. Sprint 8 is 20 minutes, three-times-a-week.

Athlete or middle-aged adult, or senior living home resident, as human beings, all of us have *fast-muscle fiber* in our muscle composition all our lives. We have it there for a reason. Most people just let the fast fiber atrophy (grow smaller) simply because they don't use it.

The great thing about *fast-muscle fiber* is that you don't have to spend a lot of time exercising. *Fast-muscle fiber* isn't meant for endurance. It's meant to run a 60-meter sprint, steal second base, make a game-winning tackle or score a touchdown. It's meant to get a comprehensive workout in a short amount of time.

Actually, it's a mistake trying to spend a lot of time in the gym. When you work *all three muscle-fiber types*, it doesn't take a lot of time. When people use the traditional, *slow-muscle fiber* training cardio, the way they get progressive overload for results to continue is by going longer, and longer. The mistake of only working half the muscle fiber (the *slow-muscle fiber*) means poor results even after hours and hours of training (unless you starve).

People using the long / slow method of cardio seem to become complacent with less than desirable results. Sadly, many blame themselves for their perceived failure because they didn't starve enough to see any changes. I think many of these people become the January 1 -15th crowd.

They never see or feel real results, and it becomes easy for them to quit. They quit or they begin to accept a level of fitness and strength far, far less than their potential -- simply because they chose the wrong tool.

When doing cardio, it doesn't take a long time to reach the *fast-muscle fiber* for great results, but fast-fiber has to be recruited the right way during exercise to reduce the risk of injury and to achieve the huge release of exercise-induced growth hormone.

Sprint 8 is a very specific formula that can be done in many different ways. Sprint 8 is the only commercially researched and tested cardio program designed to release the most growth hormone possible, to get the best results possible in the shortest amount of time.

Growth hormone is the ultimate FITNESS HORMONE because it promotes muscular definition while reducing fat

Thomas C. Welbourne, Ph.D. (2002, *Boost Your Growth Hormone Output Through Amino Acid Supplements*, LSU Medical Center Dept. of Molecular Cellular Physiology

The Sprint 8 Cardio Protocol can be performed in many different ways

3

Exercise-Induced Growth Hormone

One of the key factors in the condition of the human body is human growth hormone and its role in your physique's condition. Many people seem to be unaware of the role that growth hormone plays in the condition of the body. Growth hormone is vital to the body's status at any point in time. This substance is what makes the body grow in height

Growth hormone is one of the most powerful hormones in the human body. It can cause an increase in muscle and at the same time, it can decrease body fat percentage. The powerful combination of dropping body fat while adding muscle at the same time is highly beneficial to the body.

Youth is the one time when human growth hormone is in abundant supply in the body. Ever wonder why a teenage athlete can eat horrible and still have lots of muscle and be ripped? Growth hormone is a key reason why.

After you reach your late teens, growth hormone declines rapidly, and it continues to drop as you age. In fact, the decline of growth hormone in the body mirrors the aging process very closely. The only people that defy the aging calendar are sprinting sports athletes that continue to train their *fast-muscle fiber* and therefore continue achieving huge releases of growth hormone.

Most people suffer from the middle-age spread. We have laughed about it, but every middle-age adult knows the truth. This is a real condition. We hear people saying things like, *Everything I eat turns to fat*, and *My metabolism is slowing down*. Researchers have given this condition a name, *somatopause*.

Somatopause - The Decline of Growth Hormone

There is a name for the condition that strikes middle-age adults. Researchers call it the somatopause. The dictionary definition is *a gradual and progressive decrease in growth hormone secretion that occurs normally with increasing age during adult life and is associated with an increase in adipose tissue and LDL levels and a decrease in lean body mass*, (Merriam-Webster).

Somatopause is not positive. It has the nasty effect of adding fat, increasing bad cholesterol and destroying lean muscle. In other words, it really messes up your body. You see the effects of somatopause as people age - they carry more body fat and the muscles seem to shrink and disappear. Somatopause causes the body to start to fall apart.

As shown in the graphic, this condition begins in the mid-30s, and it's tied directly to the way the body declines in its natural production of growth hormone during aging.

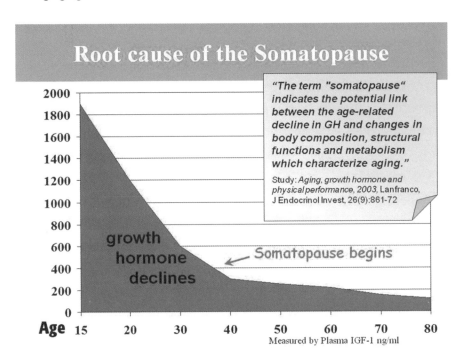

There is a Natural Cure

There are two realistic cures for the middle-age somatopause. You can inject growth hormone. The results in the research are impressive. But it doesn't take rocket-science to figure out that injecting a hormone daily without exercise or dieting will eventually lead to a price-to-pay in terms of unwanted, long-term side effects that we reviewed in Chapter 1.

Thousands of people have spent a lot of money injecting growth hormone. A Harvard Medical School publication, *Harvard Men's Health Watch* reported that as many as *20,000 to 30,000 have used growth hormone as "anti-aging" therapy and as many as 100,000 people have injected growth hormone without a valid prescription in one year,* (*Growth hormone, athletic performance, and aging.* Harvard Men's Health Watch May 1, 2010).

Growth Hormone injections aren't cheap. Authors for *ABCnewstogo.com* estimated the cost of growth hormone injections to be $8,000 to $10,000 per year, (Canning, A, (Aug, 9 2011). *HGH, Human Growth Hormone, Injections Give Couple New Energy, Enjoyment of Life,* , http://abcnews.go.com/Health/hgh-human-growth-hormone-injections-give-couple-energy/story?id=14260228).

But even if you can afford the injections, wouldn't the natural way of increasing growth hormone through exercise be the first method attempted -- at least to see if it works or not?

It's not the purpose of this book to slam anti-aging physicians or the thousands that go to anti-aging physicians for growth hormone injections. The purpose of this book is to encourage you to try the natural method of increasing growth hormone by giving Sprint 8 a personal eight-week experiment.

For every medical condition, I can show you a study where exercise will benefit the condition.

- Dr. Shail Singh, President, Excel Medicine Inc.

Dr. Singh is a board-certified physician in Internal Medicine and Hospice & Palliative Medicine and Medical Director for the Sprint 8 Challenge
www.excelmedicine.com

Growth Hormone Attacks Somatopause

There is some good news about somatopause. You can delay it and even stop it. The somatopause symptoms are part of the aging process of the human body, but it can be halted and even reversed.

You don't have to succumb to somatopause's cruel attempt to turn your body into a fat, muscle-less ball of bad cholesterol. There is a way to beat somatopause. It is possible to get into a lean and mean condition even after you have spent several years under somatopause's spell.

Age is not a barrier. You can attack somatopause at any age. In fact, the results of beating somatopause are often the most dramatic in older people. Many people who have employed Sprint 8 training have been able to sideline somatopause and realize some incredible results in their personal training.

Sprint 8 Cardio attacks the somatopause at its core roots. And you are only taking 20 minutes, three-days-a-week to combat it naturally.

Flipping the Growth Hormone Switch

It isn't necessary to risk your health to achieve significant growth hormone action because the beneficial effects of Sprint 8 can actually mimic the effects of growth hormone treatment. However, this isn't a blanket statement for all exercise.

Only a very specific type of exercise can act as a natural stimulant of a significant release of growth hormone. That's exactly what this book is all about. I want to show you how to successfully flip on the growth hormone switch so you can get the benefits of increasing this powerful hormone. The Sprint 8 Cardio Protocol is the most natural way possible.

GH Serum-Level
Pre-Sprint 8 to Post Sprint 8

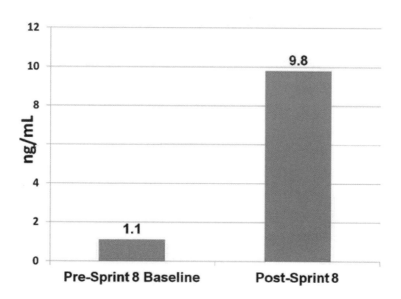

Very Specific Cardio Protocol

All exercise is beneficial for the body, but not all exercise has a significant impact on growth hormone release. You have to reach *all four* benchmarks.

In order to strongly stimulate the growth hormone response, the workout has to cause mission-critical responses in the body. To ensure the intensity is great enough to accomplish the task, it must consist of several specific elements. When these elements occur in response to the exercise, the body releases a significant amount of growth hormone. And it stays elevated for around two hours, going after body fat like a heat seeking missile.

Research at the University of Virginia demonstrates exercise increases the amount of growth hormone in a linear relationship to the intensity of exercise. There are four specific elements that must exist for human growth hormone to be effectively released during exercise. These benchmarks include *oxygen debt, increased body temperature, muscle burn* and *adrenal response*.

Benchmark 1: Oxygen Debt

Oxygen debt is self explanatory -- your body is pushed to the point where it demands more oxygen, and you get really winded. This state is unique to high-intensity anaerobic training.

Finish a jog and you aren't necessarily out of breath. Doing a Sprint 8 rep the right way -- an all-out cardio sprint where you are going as hard-as-you-can and as fast-as-you-can, so hard and fast you can't possibly make it longer than 30 seconds -- your body immediately switches to a state of desperately needing more oxygen.

There is a noticeable response in your body as it requires more oxygen and you definitely feel it. Research shows oxygen debt plays an important role in causing the body to release exercise-induced growth hormone, (Vanhelder. (1987) *Regulation of growth hormone during exercise by oxygen demand and availability.*

Oxygen debt can be created in several ways. A maximum-intensity anaerobic sprint on a typical cardio unit you see in most fitness centers today -- where you attempt maximum output but can't hold it longer than 30 seconds -- will get you oxygen deprived. Doing all-out sprint running or swimming gets the job done. The all-out sprint running only goes for 8 to 12 seconds and covers 70 yards on a football field. Sprint swimming is an all-out, fast-as-you-can swim sprint of 25 meters. Either approach will put you into oxygen debt quickly. There is no way of missing this growth hormone release mark -- you will be gasping for air.

When running the Sprint 8, please note that unlike using cardio units in the fitness center that are safer on the hamstrings than sprint running, it takes 6 to 8 weeks, and even longer to progressively build the *fast-muscle fiber* in the hamstrings, calves and achilles tendons that propel sprint running.

When running sprints, you are taking your entire body weight and with each step, you are generating a huge amount of force directly on your hamstrings to throw your body several feet forward with each step. I'll discuss this more in the following chapter.

The bottom line on oxygen debt is simple -- either an exercise causes this reaction or it doesn't. Walking, even jogging does *not* produce noticeable oxygen debt for most healthy people. Cardio sprinting on the other hand, immediately causes oxygen debt on the first repetition. The more intense the exercise, the more it will cause oxygen debt.

Benchmark 2: Increased Body Temperature

A higher body temperature is another factor necessary for exercise-induced growth hormone release, (Vigas. *Role of body temperature in exercise-induced growth hormone and prolactin release in non-trained and physically fit subjects,* 2000).

Researchers report:

> *This study demonstrated that exercising in the cold can diminish the exercise-induced systemic inflammatory response seen in a thermoneutral environment,* (Gagnon D. (2014, OCT 22) *The effects of cold exposure on leukocytes, hormones and cytokines during acute exercise in humans.* Oct 22;9(10).

In an earlier study, researchers demonstrated that growth hormone won't release when exercise occurs in a cold room where body temperature can't be increased, (Christensen. (1984) *Characterization of growth hormone release in response to external heating: Comparison to exercise induced release*).

Increasing body temperature is one of the four major thresholds that need to be achieved to release growth hormone. Researchers report that *when a certain threshold is exceeded, a hormonal response is induced,* (Wahl P. (2013 Dec, 23) *Effects of active vs. passive recovery during Wingate-based training on the acute hormonal, metabolic and psychological response.* Growth Horm IGF Res(6):201-8).

The takeaway for Sprint 8 Benchmark 2 is getting the body temperature to increase. It is not necessary for a huge increase as even a small increase can get the ball rolling. However, you can't take it for granted. You want your training to heat things up a bit to enhance the environment for growth hormone activity. Doing a maximum intensity, cardio sprint for 30 seconds will certainly heat your body up very quickly unless you are in an extreme cold environment.

Benchmark 3: Muscle Burn

Muscle burn ties in to the oxygen debt part of training that forces the pituitary to release significant amounts of growth hormone. The *burn* in your muscles is actually the muscles becoming acidic when they are working at maximal levels.

This is the painful feeling you get in the muscles when you push them hard. It's unmistakable. Growth hormone release begins within minutes of reaching the muscle burning lactate threshold benchmark during exercise, (Vanhelder (1984) *Growth hormone responses during intermittent weight lifting exercise in men*).

The *muscle burn* isn't a good feeling, but it's a great barometer telling you *now this exercise is productive.* The science behind this is important to understand. Your muscles don't reach an acidic, muscle-burning state from low-intensity exercise -- you have to take your body to a high level of intensity to get the benefits of exercise-induced growth hormone.

I frequently explain during strength training, *it's just a warm up until the muscles start burning. It's how many reps you do after the burn begins that gets the results*. It's when you push the muscles past the initial burning phase that you get the best adaptation to training.

Researchers reported in early studies that the lactic acid in muscles may be partly responsible for growth hormone release during anaerobic exercise, (Gordon. (1994, Feb) *Effect of acid-base balance on the growth hormone response to acute high-intensity cycle exercise*, J Appl Physiol 1;76(2):821-9.).

Later studies support these findings, *lactate could play a major role in the EIGR (exercise-induced growth hormone)*, (Godfrey RJ, (2009 Jul) *Exercise-induce growth hormone) in humans, (The role of lactate in the exercise-induced human growth hormone response: evidence from McArdle disease*. Br J Sports Med. ;43(7).

It was once thought the buildup of lactic acid caused muscle soreness. Not true. Lactic acid is recycled in the body before soreness appears and used for energy somewhat like a ventless fireplace burns gas. Soreness is caused by numerous muscle micro-tears, or overstretching the muscle during exercise. Soreness should not be considered as an indicator of muscle damage. Soreness should be seen as a sign of the regenerative process, which increases muscle mass, (Coudreuse JM.(2004 Aug) *Delayed post effort muscle soreness.* Ann Readapt Med Phys.;47(6):290-8).

Benchmark 4: Adrenal Response

The final key element in the growth hormone response is related to other benchmarks that maximum-effort, sprint-intensity cardio produces -- the adrenal response. The increase of growth hormone during exercise is closely correlated with the release of adrenal hormones (adrenaline and norepinephrine). This occurs after reaching the muscles burning *lactate threshold* benchmark, (Pritzlaff. (1999) *Impact of acute exercise intensity on pulsatile growth hormone release in men,* J Appl Physiol and *Threshold increases in plasma growth hormone*).

Exercise must be very intense in order to stimulate the production of an epinephrine response necessary for growth hormone release. The Sprint 8 Cardio Protocol will take you to this level every time -- if you do it correctly.

Four Benchmarks for Growth Hormone Release
1. **Oxygen debt** (out-of-breath response)
2. **Lactic acid** (muscles burning response)
3. **Increased body temperature**
4. **Adrenal response** (slightly painful)

Achieving the adrenal response has far-reaching positives for improving health. A major new, landmark study that's shocking the world of cancer care is directly related to the adrenal response from sprint-intensity cardio in mice. More about this exciting new study in Chapter 5, *Benefits of Sprint 8.*

Dr. Len Kravitz reports this level of cardio intensity can increase norepinephrine by 6 - 14 times greater than baseline, (Kravitz, L. (2014). *Metabolic effects of HIIT.* IDEA Fitness Journal, 11(5), 16-18).

Dr. Stephen Boutcher reports healthy young men, older adult men, and women *can improve their cardiorespiratory fitness as much as 46 percent in less than 15 weeks,* (Boutcher, S.H. (2011), *High-Intensity Intermittent Exercise and Fat Loss.* J Obes.868305. PMC2991639).

Growth Hormone Release

Put these four elements together and you ensure that you achieve the benchmarks for a maximum release of growth hormone. The question is what specifically causes these four benchmark elements to exist together, synergistically stimulating growth hormone? How can you hit all four elements at once?

Sprint-intensity cardio is the answer to the question. And the Sprint 8 Cardio Protocol is the specific tool proven and tested to turn on the growth hormone release switch by achieving these necessary benchmarks. You can't turn on the growth hormone release switch sitting on the sofa or doing magazine-reading paced cardio. It takes a very specific tool to get you there.

Specific Type of Cardio

Sprint-intensity cardio is the key to reaching the four benchmarks that cause growth hormone production. However, there is a big caveat -- not just any exercise will do. Traditional exercise, such as going out for a jog or getting in a long walk, will burn off a few calories but it won't get the job done. Neither will pumping a few moderate dumbbells.

That's why people who just rely on jogging or similar activity as a training tool come up short of reaching their full potential. They don't overcome the negative *slope of the somatopause* trend because growth hormone is not activated at any significant amount.

The body's critical mass is not exploited at maximum levels so the metabolism and hormones don't peak. Burning calories from exercise is great, but if you really want to change your body you have to reverse the slope of the somatopause. It is crucial to attack somatopause because it has such a huge effect on the condition of your body. *Attack* is the way to think about it. Just *working on it* won't get it done. You need an attack mind-set to do the Sprint 8 Cardio Protocol correctly. But the *attack* is in 30 seconds or less with 90-seconds afterwards to recover. I have never met anyone who believes they can't go intense for 30 seconds.

This is where the battle is won or lost! To fight somatopause you need a lot more than traditional, moderate-paced cardio. What you need is the common denominator found in reaching all four benchmarks for growth hormone release and that is *sprint-intensity* found in the Sprint 8 Cardio Protocol.

Slow-moving exercise, and even moderate-intensity cardio, will not clear the growth hormone stimulation hurdles. But maximum effort, sprint-intensity for 30-seconds will. Researchers report:

> *Sprint interval training (SIT) involving repeated 30-s "all out" efforts have resulted in significantly improved skeletal muscle oxidative capacity, maximal oxygen uptake, and endurance performance.* The ***positive impact of SIT on cardiorespiratory fitness has far-reaching health implications,*** (Gist N. (2014, Feb) *Sprint interval training effects on aerobic capacity: a systematic review and meta analysis.* Sports Med. 44 (2):269-79).

Sprint-Intensity for Short Duration

The type of training requisite for meeting the four key benchmarks of growth hormone release is training that achieves sprint intensity for very specific, short durations. In order to reach the full potential of your body at any age and receive all the benefits from this wonderful hormone, you must train with maximum intensity for brief periods.

The role of sprint-intensity exercise cannot be overstated as it is critical for a large release of exercise-induced growth hormone release and positive change for your body.

There are two reasons for always making sprint-intensity training the key component of your workout schedule. The first is the necessity of releasing exercise-induced growth hormone. The second is the necessity of working the *fast-twitch muscle fibers* so the training is comprehensive. Together they add up to radically change your body for the better.

Researchers report in the *Journal of Sports Science; The duration of a bout of **maximal sprint exercise determines the magnitude of the GH response,*** (Journal of Sports Science, June 2002).

The 90-second Active Recovery

In between each cardio sprint is a period of active recovery. This is 90 seconds of active recovery, not cardio. You keep moving (active) but at a slow recovery pace. You are trying to recover at the pace of a casual-paced walk.

Very important; don't try to make the 90 seconds lower-intensity cardio. Keep it active recovery. Trying to make this cardio rather than active recovery will keep you from getting adequately recovered, and this means you won't be able to go all-out on the following cardio sprint.

Some people who have tried to copy the Sprint 8, change it to rush the active recovery. This is a huge mistake. I have tested 30, 60, 90-second recovery periods. And by far, the 90-second recovery is so much more demanding.

The reason for this is simple. You can't get recovered enough to do the following cardio sprint with all-out sprint intensity unless you recover for the *full* 90 seconds.

A 60-second active recovery may allow you to only do two high-quality, cardio-sprint reps, and a 30-second recovery makes the program nothing more than low-intensity interval training after the first cardio-sprint rep.

The only interval training in the Sprint 8 Cardio Protocol is the active recovery. Sprint 8 is all-out sprint cardio, and it is much more intense than the interval training practiced today. Sprint 8 Cardio compared to interval training that most people do is college to kindergarten apart in intensity and results.

No matter how well you are conditioned, your *fast-muscle fiber* is not recovered when you shorten the 90-second recovery. While it seems like a shorter recovery would be harder and better, it is just the opposite.

Shortening the 90-second recovery makes it easier because your heart muscle doesn't have to oxygenate the fast fiber that's not fully recovered and not being recruited. Shortening it will keep you from doing sprint intensity. Shortening the active recovery will make it a cardio-coasting, low-intensity interval training workout. Researchers report:

> *It appears that this kind of exercise protocol with **Active Recovery phases between the intervals may promote anabolic processes**,* (Wahl P, (2014) *Active vs. passive recovery during high-intensity training influences hormonal response.* Int J Sports Med. Jun;35(7):583-9).

Case Study, Martha Bejarano

Martha Bejarano's friends would describe her as *into fitness.* Frequently, she would do a boot camp two days-a-week, lift weights with a trainer, and then run afterwards to train for several half marathons a year.

Living in the beautiful Bay Area of California, at age 50 and training 5 to 6 days a week, sometimes 2 and 3 hours a day, Martha was getting all the results possible. All the results from functional boot camp training, strength training with weights, and running mileage. Yet, she still wanted to reduce body fat, improve fitness, and lose the last *stubborn pounds* without starving because she knew losing weight with diet may slow down her metabolism. And she didn't want to lose ground she already gained.

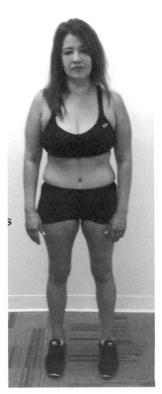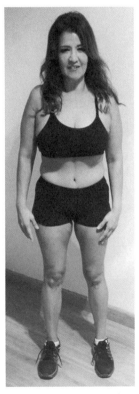

She signed up for the *Sprint 8 Challenge*, an 8-week course with Sprint 8 on an elliptical or recumbent bike to start the class and to accomplish a natural injection for growth hormone. Once growth hormone is circulating in the blood stream from the Sprint 8 Protocol, the class would do 25 minutes of strength training with *E-Lift technique* on push and press exercise movements (covered in detail in *Ready, Set, Go! Fitness*) to target all three *muscle-fiber types* during strength training. Then class would finish with the *10-Minute Stretching Routine* (also covered in *Ready, Set, Go! Fitness*).

Even though Martha would be considered to be in top condition for most 50-year old women, she tapped into the synergistic impact of exercise-induced growth hormone released with Sprint 8 and achieved amazing results.

She lost those six pounds in eight weeks without changing her already clean moderation diet. Her body fat dropped 44 pounds to 38 pounds while increasing her muscle mass from 57.3 pounds to 57.7 pounds of lean mass. Martha's trunk body fat dropped from 24 pounds to 21 pounds. This is evident in the *before* and *after* photos.

Weight 148

Weight 142

Martha's cholesterol health improved during the eight weeks. Her bad LDL's dropped 31 points (a 23% drop). And her good HDL's increased by 10 points.

4

The Ultimate Driver of Sprint Intensity

Muscle Fiber Recruitment

The ultimate driver of sprint-intensity training that evokes a release of huge amounts of growth hormone naturally is the kind of cardio that will recruit both types of *fast-twitch muscle fiber* for a very specific and tested number of seconds, 30 seconds. Please note, the most important part of this protocol is the exact amount of active recovery in between each cardio sprint, 90 seconds.

The typical person in a gym is only working *slow-twitch muscle fibers*. That's not negative since approximately half your muscle fiber is composed of *slow-muscle fiber*. However, your body is composed of more than just *slow-twitch muscle*. In order for you to truly train your body, it is essential to comprehensively train all three *muscle-fiber types*.

Training half the body will only produce a body that is halfway in shape. A half trained body won't come near to the total development you have the potential to reach. Training all the muscle fibers -- *slow, fast* and *super-fast fiber* -- will help transform your body much quicker, and release a huge amount of exercise-induced growth hormone so it can work its body fat cutting, muscle building magic in the body.

Most cardio programs today as well as many strength training programs are based on very old school science that treats muscle as one fiber type, *slow-twitch type I* muscle. Many strength exercises and programs today that are titled as *new and innovative* are still based on the old science of working *slow-muscle fiber*.

While some new programs and exercises add stability or balance training with cables, bands and suspension units, and some change angles for variety or marketing purposes, they are still based on *slow-muscle fiber* development.

The Sprint 8 Cardio Protocol is *not* one of those programs. Sprint 8 was created to target exercise-induced growth hormone -- to listen to how the body is telling us how to exercise. Discoveries about muscle fiber recruitment has guided the Sprint 8 tool development process.

Muscle-fiber recruitment has totally changed the way we should think about training. Distinguished researcher Dr. Edward Coyle reports:

> *In fact, the low-intensity aerobic exercise that is typically prescribed for endurance training or health is not very effective at increasing aerobic enzyme activity in type II muscle fibers, which comprise approximately one-half of the fibers within the thigh (vastus) and calf (gastrocnemius) muscle in most people.* ***Thus low-intensity aerobic training is not a very effective or efficient method for maximizing aerobic adaptations in skeletal muscle because it generally does not recruit type II muscle fibers,*** (Coyle, (2005) Journal of Applied Physiology).

Muscle Recruitment

As a speed technique coach, I live in a world of *super-fast muscle fiber* recruitment and very specific training to target *IIx fast-twitch muscle fiber*. This is necessary to get athletes faster for sport-specific and position-specific movements. I constantly see this lesson over-and-over with athletes at all levels, even professional athletes. The body always tries to do things with *slow-twitch muscle fiber* in the endurance energy system.

This is a fundamental fact that you need to internalize and understand before you do Sprint 8, otherwise you probably will not do it correctly. **The body always tries to do things with *slow-twitch muscle fiber* in the endurance energy system.**

Your brain thinks it is doing you a big favor *not* to recruit *fast-muscle fiber*. One more time, Your brain thinks it is doing you a big favor *not* to recruit *fast-muscle fiber.* Your brain is trying to conserve *fast-twitch fiber* and not use it, in case you need this muscle fiber fresh and ready to run away from a bad guy.

For this reason, it's very important for you to know and understand that the brain always tries to find the easiest way to do an exercise, so you can endure and not necessarily get the best workout in the shortest amount of time.

This is essential to know. You must understand muscle fiber recruitment science and the natural tendency of the body to always do things with slow-muscle fiber in the endurance energy system. Otherwise, you won't consistently reach for the intensity level required to get the best results.

Muscle recruitment works like this. The brain essentially sends the *slow-twitch muscle fiber* to accomplish a task in the endurance energy system so you can endure all day. However, when your brain senses that you are moving really fast, your brain sends messages through your nervous system to the *IIa fast-muscle* (the muscle fiber that moves five times faster than the slow) to be recruited and help make the movement.

When you are moving at maximum speed and intensity with all-out effort, the brain now sends messages to the *super-fast IIx muscle fiber* (that moves ten times faster than the slow) to jump in and help add strength and speed to the movement.

The reason muscle fiber type science is so important to the success of Sprint 8 is because the more muscle fiber you recruit during the cardio sprint, the harder your heart muscle and lungs have to work to oxygenate *all three muscle-fiber groups* propelling the movement. *Fast-fiber* recruitment is the ultimate driver behind the maximum-effort, all-out, sprint-intensity cardio program in this book.

It's well known you get exercise intensity from three sources; the amount of resistance, duration, and most importantly for the principles in this book, velocity of movement. But it can't be a blind velocity, that's too easy. Sometimes in spin class for example, there can be easy velocity with little resistance. In Sprint 8, each cardio sprint has to be hard and fast. And the goal is a balance of the two, hard and fast.

For your cardio sprint to count as a Sprint 8 cardio sprint, it has to be more than just hard and fast. It has to be as hard and fast as you can go. Important point: if you can possibly go longer than 30 seconds, don't count it. It means you have paced during that cardio sprint.

It has to be so intense (by going as hard and as fast as you can), that you can't go longer than 30 seconds.

> **NOTE: If you can go longer than 30-seconds during a cardio sprint, you paced** and pacing means you didn't recruit all three muscle-fiber types to propel the exercise and your lungs, and your heart muscle didn't work at maximum-effort, sprint-intensity required for Sprint 8.

Sprint 8 seeks to find a balance of resistance and velocity of movement for a short, maximum-effort, cardio sprint duration of 30 seconds or less, which forces recruitment of all three muscle fiber types. Researchers report on the tremendous benefit of recruiting all three muscle-fiber types that occurs with maximum-effort, sprint-intensity cardio:

> **Exercise programs that engage as much skeletal muscle mass, and recruit as many muscle fibers within each muscle, as possible will generate the greatest improvements** in microvascular function, providing the duration of the stimulus is sufficient. Primary improvements in microvascular function occur in tissues (skeletal muscle primarily) engaged during exercise and secondary improvements in microvascular function throughout the body may result from improved blood glucose control.... vigorous intensity exercise programs is not simply "more is better." Rather, the additional benefit is the result of exercise-induced adaptations in and around more muscle fibers, resulting in more muscle mass, and the associated microvasculature, being changed, (Oliver TD. (2015 Sep) Endurance vs. interval sprint training and/or resistance training; impact on microvascular dysfunction in type 2 diabetes. Am J Physiol Heart Circ Physiol.00440).

Sprint-intensity Builds Endurance

In my opinion, one of the main reasons we have the obesity epidemic is due to the past failure of applying the science of muscle-fiber recruitment with exercise, programming and sports performance training. In essence, society says *now that you are older and through playing sports, now that you are an adult throw all of your fast-muscle fiber out the window and go jog a marathon.*

Trainers and coaches frequently fall into an incorrect mode of thinking the way to build endurance is to do longer duration training with progressively shorter recovery periods. Listen, endurance doesn't come from training long hours. Endurance comes from the mitochondria in the muscle cells that produce ATP energy in the body. The number one way to increase mitochondria is fast-fiber recruiting, maximum-effort, sprint-intensity cardio.

Endurance doesn't come from doing longer and longer runs. Frequently, endurance athletes improve their time performance when they do frequent long duration training because they aren't eating and they lose weight. Their time improvement is because they are carrying less mass. They aren't getting stronger, they're simply carrying less mass. This can be misleading to endurance athletes and coaches because this will get small improvements in performance times. This method of improving endurance also leads to stress-related overtraining injury issues and a calendar with no time for family or friends.

If endurance athletes trained based on improving endurance with the scientific method of increasing mitochondria (the source of ATP energy) in a balanced approach of event-specific endurance training and speed training to increase mitochondria, performance will improve. It improves because all three muscle fiber types are being strengthened and injury risk from overtraining is reduced. There's also more time for family and friends.

I have seen this first hand with a Kenyan training for the college cross-country season. As a freshman running against far more experienced runners in his first college season, Nelphat Bor used the mitochondria training approach, improved, and won the conference collegiate championship while pursing a nursing degree and working part time. Nelphat improved his performance and ran a 5K in 16.03 and a 8K in 26.33.

Mitochondria researcher, George F. Schreiner M.D., Ph.D. and CEO of Cardero Therapeutics, explained some key information that hasn't made it to the mainstream literature. Dr. Schreiner explains *fast-muscle fiber* does not have a lot of mitochondria. *Fast-muscle fiber (IIa)* has 20 percent less mitochondria than the *slow-muscle fiber (type I)*, and the *super-fast muscle fiber (IIx)* has 50 percent less than the *slow-muscle fiber.*

Dr. Schreiner explains when both types of *fast-muscle fiber* are recruited and worked (like we do in Sprint 8), the brain sends messengers to the *slow-muscle fiber* to start producing mitochondria like crazy.

Research shows *fast-twitch muscle* training close to *100 percent intensity* was enough to roughly *triple mitochondria* output in 8 weeks. This process starts immediately and doesn't take long. Dr. John Holloszy is the *Father of High Intensity Training*, and his pioneering research shows mitochondria in muscle cells can increase in number by 50 percent in only a few weeks.

The bottom line is you cannot reach your full physical potential unless you work both types of *fast-twitch muscle fiber* on a consistent basis. When you are working the *fast-muscle fiber*, the *slow Type I fiber* hasn't stopped working. *Slow (Type I) fiber* continues working at the same time. When you recruit a lot more muscle fiber, your heart muscle has to work harder to send blood to those muscles to oxygenate the cells so you can keep going.

The most important thing you can do for your fitness improvement is different than most people think. True fitness has two parts. True fitness is conditioning the *aerobic process* AND *anaerobic process* of the heart muscle. The anaerobic process is how the heart muscle works when it is working very hard at the highest levels of intensity without getting enough oxygen.

Doing the Sprint 8 Cardio Protocol with maximum-effort, sprint-intensity during the 30-second cardio sprints will condition both processes of the heart muscle, aerobic and anaerobic.

Sprint 8 Strengthens Muscle & Skeleton

Sprint-intensity cardio will build your *fast-twitch muscle fiber.* This helps elevate your resting metabolic rate further than just focusing on traditional, long-slow, calorie-burning, *slow-muscle fiber* exercise.

When you develop both types of *fast-twitch fiber* along with developing *slow-twitch fiber,* you can achieve a much more significant fat-burning effect from your metabolic rate. This is because you are building more muscle than when you only work slow-muscle fiber.

Intensity and *fast-muscle fiber* are intrinsically linked together. Slow and moderate-paced movement will burn a few calories and strengthen slow-muscle fiber, but these levels of intensity won't work the anaerobic process of your heart muscle for superior results unless you train for hours and hours.

Sprint 8 is great for your bones. Just ask any orthopedic physician about the skeleton damage that is done by doing hours and hours of long-slow running (when you don't run fast enough to strike the surface mid-foot). When running distances fast enough to strike the surface mid-foot, the pounding is not felt straight down the skeleton like it is with slow running that strikes the surface heel toe. If someone has a light frame, trained in running technique, and runs fast enough to strike the surface mid foot, these people can generally run distance safely for years.

Someone mid weight or heavy weight, who runs slow enough to strike the surface heel toe is forcing the skeleton to receive a lot more force than the skeleton of the light weight trained runner. Some pounding the pavement can be positive on building bone density in the legs. However, the moment the weakest muscle in the leg gets fatigued, these runners will still be working their heart muscle (good), but sacrificing their skeleton in the process (bad).

Muscle is connected to the bones at two different insertion points. Take your biceps for example. These muscles are connected to bone near your shoulder and at your elbow. When you do a bicep curl, the muscle flexes to move. This action forces the muscle to tug at the bone in two places. Now the bone (in a positive way) is being stressed so you are working the muscle and the bone at the same time. Just like muscle takes protein and nutrients to build muscle when we sleep, now the bones that were stressed with exercise will need calcium and minerals to build thicker and stronger bones when we sleep.

Important point: Taking calcium and bone building supplements to make bones thicker and stronger without stressing the bones with exercise is like going to the gas pump, paying for gas, but missing the hole. Too much pounding the payment can be harmful, but not stressing your bones with exercise, especially strength training, means bones will continue to get smaller and smaller and weaker and weaker.

The Sprint 8 Cardio Protocol performed correctly will force all three *muscle-fiber types* to generate significant force and tug at the bones in your legs. Your leg muscles, tendons, ligaments and bones get worked so they will adapt by getting stronger.

Time Element

The sprint-intensity factor is one of two vital inputs you need to control the release of exercise-induced growth hormone in your body. The other factor is time. How long you train is a critical issue for any training style and is especially important when it comes to growth hormone release. The timing factor plays an essential role in how your body responds to exercise stimulation.

To achieve all that the body has to offer from your time investment in exercise, it is imperative to train targeting *fast-fiber* recruitment with maximum effort, bursts of sprint-intensity cardio aimed at a goal of 30 *all-out* seconds. Remember, if you can go longer than 30 seconds, don't count that rep. You have paced and pacing is the enemy of intensity and exercise-induced growth hormone release.

On a typical piece of cardio equipment, an elliptical for example, you warm up for two minutes on an easy level, Level 1 or 2. Five seconds before the cardio sprint start mark, put the unit to up to level 8 to 12. Then sprint with arms and legs all-out, fast-as-you-can aiming for a full 30-second cardio sprint.

If the cardio sprint was really hard to make 30 seconds, or if you just couldn't go past 26 seconds before your legs started to slow down, congratulations. You did it right!

After the cardio sprint, drop the resistance level down to level 1 again for a *full* 90-second active recovery, which should be the intensity level of a casual-paced walk. Five seconds before the second 30-second cardio sprint, put it up to the same resistance level as the last cardio sprint. It takes a few workouts to get the hang of the levels. Just do two to four segments.

Doesn't sound too bad so far, does it? For most people two reps is a great starting place. Very few people, no matter how fit and conditioned they are, can do five reps correctly the first time. The goal isn't to do all 8 reps. The goal is to do each one correctly, and over time, build up to all 8 reps.

20-Minutes, three-times-a-week

How long is the Sprint 8 Protocol when I build up to all 8 reps? Initially, you start with two to four Sprint 8 reps and slowly build to all 8 reps. This can take several weeks or even months to achieve. That's positive.

You should be releasing significant amounts of growth hormone on just two reps. Over time, the goal is to build up to the fully mature Sprint 8, which is all 8 reps and a two minute cool down.

In my 30 plus years of preaching Sprint 8, I have only seen a few people ever do all 8 reps correctly the first time. I can almost guarantee that people who do marathons and ultra 100-mile events will not be able to do all 8 reps correctly. The reason why is simple. They practice hours and hours *not* recruiting *fast-muscle fiber* so they oxygenate less muscle fiber and endure longer. And they *don't* condition the anaerobic process of their heart muscle, which is an entirely different process.

When it comes to Sprint 8 cardio, longer is not better. In fact, longer is bad! The fully mature Sprint 8 Protocol on an elliptical, recumbent bike, upright bike or treadmill is 8 reps and totals 20 minutes (when you add the two-minute warm up and two-minute cool down and take 90 seconds for the active recovery in between each cardio sprint).

If you think you ever need to do more than 8 reps, you didn't do it correctly. In my 30 plus years teaching Sprint 8, I've never had anyone who does Sprint 8 correctly say just before rep number 6, *I think I'll do one more today.* This doesn't happen.

There is a caveat for the 20-minute mark however. Of the 20-minute program, only 4 minutes needs to be in an all-out mode of 30 seconds of as-hard-as-you-can-go, *fast-fiber* recruiting, you can't-go-any-harder-or-faster sprint intensity. If you do each Sprint 8 rep the right way, you will never need to do more than 8 reps.

A 20 minute workout may seem like an easy thing to do, but when you try it, you'll see that sprint-intensity cardio is tough. The fully mature Sprint 8 with all 8 reps is very demanding to say the least. It's tough. But it produces the best results humanly possible from cardio exercise in body fat reduction and endurance energy building. You should physically feel the energy boost after a couple of Sprint 8 workouts.

Can you commit to 20 minutes, three-days-a-week for an 8-week personal experiment? If you will make that commitment, you will physically see and feel the results. You will feel more energy during the day. This isn't a placebo. It's real. It's real because you are changing your body at the cellular level to have more mitochondria that produces energy (ATP) in our bodies.

You will feel your clothes fitting looser within a couple of weeks. You should also feel stronger. The benefits of increasing growth hormone are huge. This is why growth hormone injections are banned for athletes. It makes athletes stronger and improves performance. Sprint 8 does the job NATURALLY.

Post Workout Effect

Growth hormone release begins earlier in the Protocol, but it's at the 16 to 20-minute mark that the body realizes a significant release of growth hormone, which continues to elevate even after the workout is over, and peaks at roughly one hour into the post workout time frame.

Growth hormone stays significantly elevated for two hours after Sprint 8, targeting after body fat like a heat-seeking missile. This gives you a two-hour **Synergy Window** for exercise-induced growth hormone to continue circulating in your body to do its body-fat cutting, muscle building, ATP energy-doubling work inside your body.

Human Growth Hormone is the most powerful anabolic stimulus known to science

- Dr. Michael Colgan, The Sports Nutrition Guide

Sprint 8 Two-Hour Synergy Window

Firing up the growth hormone release process with the Sprint 8 Cardio Protocol has the extra added benefit of causing growth hormone to continue after the training is over for **two full hours of synergetic benefits --** as if you are exercising for much longer than just 20 minutes.

One study shows after peaking, exercise-induced growth hormone slowly returns to baseline, but it is significantly elevated for two hours. Another study shows that the synergistic effect of this powerful hormone will even last up to three hours, (Slias (1997) *Effects of blood pH and blood lactate on growth hormone, prolactin, and gonadotropin release after acute exercise in male volunteers*).

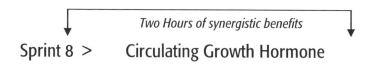

Two Hours of synergistic benefits

Sprint 8 > Circulating Growth Hormone

The *Two-Hour Synergy Window* is doing more than increasing the metabolism from a higher body temperature (that you can get with other forms of exercise or a sauna.) The *Two-Hour Synergy Window* is real and you get significant benefits from circulating growth hormone.

What most people don't know about cardio is the moment the cardio is over and the body temperature goes down, the calorie burning is over. Let me say that one more time; **the moment the cardio is over and the body temperature goes down, the calorie burning is over.**

Calorie burning is directly related to body temperature. Growth hormone releasing Sprint 8 is different. Even when body temperature goes down after Sprint 8 is over, the function of this wonderful body-fat reducing, skin thickening, muscle toning *fitness hormone,* continues to work for two full hours afterwards unless you release a counterproductive hormone called somatostatin. More on somatostatin in a coming chapter.

The ability to have high levels of growth hormone circulating for two hours afterwards has a huge, dynamic, synergistic impact on the body that is unique from any other form of exercise. The post-workout effect will maximize the benefits of the effort you put into your Sprint 8 workout.

Sprint 8 Suppresses the Hunger Hormone

Doing the Sprint 8 Protocol will suppress the hunger hormone, Ghrelin, that is released in the stomach. One thing I can promise you. After doing Sprint 8, you won't be hungry. Thinking of food after Sprint 8 will make most people nauseous.

Researchers found that when men completed HIIT training 70 minutes before a meal, their perceived appetite was lower. They ate less than the study subjects doing less intense exercise. (Sim, AY (2015) *Effects of High-Intensity Intermittent Exercise Training on Appetite Regulation.* Med Sci Sports Exerc. 2015 Nov;47(11):2441-9).

In a similar study, lead researcher Dr. David Stensel stated, *Exercise may lower levels of ghrelin, a hormone that stimulates appetite in the short term, while raising levels of peptide YY, a hormone that suppresses appetite.* (Broom DR, Stensel DJ. (2008) *Influence of resistance and aerobic exercise on hunger, circulating levels of acylated ghrelin, and peptide YY in healthy males.* Am J Physiol Regul Integr Comp Physiol. 2009 Jan;296(1):R29-35).

Suppressing the hunger hormone is positive because it makes it easier to eat less. Internationally syndicated fitness columnist James Fell states it perfectly, *Any diet that allows you to restrict calories is going to lead to weight loss. As long as you're not overeating, then all diets will work.* James writes an entertaining fitness newsletter based on mainstream facts. And he has the courage to take on the fitness fluff heads that promise results with some sort of *easy* program (www. bodyforwife.com).

Intermittent fasting is becoming recommended by many health experts based on new research. Whether it's missing a meal for a whole day, or missing a meal every now and then, there's research to show this can be positive. The hunger hormone Ghrelin tells the story behind all of this.

Ghrelin is hunger. The higher your ghrelin hormone, the more hungry you are. Reduce or suppress ghrelin, and you don't feel hungry. This makes it easier to cut back or even miss a meal.

Dr. Jason Fung has an excellent discussion of the research on fasting, which shows missing a meal or two isn't as painful as many think it will be. He writes:

> Ghrelin is the so-called hunger hormone. It was purified from rat stomach in 1999 and subsequently cloned. It binds to growth hormone (GH) secretagogue receptor, which strongly stimulates GH. So, for all you people who thought that eating makes you gain lean tissue, it is actually the opposite. Nothing turns off GH like food. Of course, food provides the nutrients needed to grow, so in fact, you need both feeding and fasting cycles to properly grow. Not all feeding, and not all fasting. Life lies in the balance of the two. The cycle of life is feast and fast.

> Ghrelin, has also been found to increase appetite and weight gain. It also antagonizes the effect of leptin (in rats at least). Leptin is the hormone produced by fat cells which turns off appetite and makes us stop eating. Ghrelin turns on appetite. So, if you want to lose weight on a long term basis, you need to tune down ghrelin.

> However, the main point of this post is to show that over intermittent and extended fasting, ghrelin, the main hormonal mediator of hunger does not increase to unmanageable levels. Rather it decreases – which is exactly what we are looking for. We want to eat less, but be more full. Fasting, unlike caloric restriction diets is the way to do that. (https:// intensivedietarymanagement.com/fasting-ghrelin-fasting-29/)

Sprint 8 suppresses the hunger hormone, ghrelin, no question. But what we don't know, does ghrelin increase two hours later and jump on us with double vengeance? I wish I could cite a study with the answer, but the truth of the matter is, exercise isn't a drug and gets very little research funding relative to drugs. If exercise were a drug, we would have tons of money for exercise research.

The most hypocritical acts seen in all of science and all of healthcare are drug companies and universities obtaining millions in grants that have to do with growth hormone, and other similar hormones, so they can make a new drug that essentially does what exercise does. Annually, millions are granted to make new drugs and very little is allocated to exercise researchers. Why? It's pretty simple, exercise isn't a drug. And this is why there is no answer to the question about ghrelin suppression time period.

I'd like to challenge the manufactures of growth hormone to fund research dollars that will at least educate people there is a natural way to increase growth hormone with sprint-intensity cardio before jumping on the injecting band wagon. It's only common sense, the first step before injecting growth hormone should be informing the patient about the benefits of exercise-induced growth hormone.

One day this will probably happen. I just hope it's voluntary and comes from pharmaceutical executive leaders who really believe their mission statements to help people. I hope it isn't the result of TV advertising to join a class-action lawsuit against drug companies failing to warn people there is a natural method to increase growth hormone.

Critical Mass

Another factor in firing up growth hormone release in the human body is the critical mass effect. When you work out with light weights, when you don't push the body hard, or when you are using exercise that is a minimal challenge to the body, you don't spark hormone release of exercise-induced hormones like testosterone, growth hormone, dopamine, and other positive hormones. Doing exercise that doesn't challenge the body is, in essence, just warming up and not really doing much. This is like showing up for work and going on a lunch break.

In order to turn on the positive hormones you get from exercise you need to move critical mass, which means it's not going to be easy. Sprint cardio on an elliptical, sprint swimming, sprint running in a park are movements of critical mass -- your entire body weight - at high speeds so it recruits a lot more muscle fiber. This puts a heavy workload on the body and acts as a critical mass marker for your body, forcing a significant hormonal response for many positive types of hormones.

Taking your body weight and riding a machine lessens intensity. However, when you add resistance back into the equation by increasing the resistance level on the machine and use sprint-intensity velocity of movement, the intensity of the exercise becomes close to the intensity of sprint running on a track, but it reduces the risk of injury to hamstrings, calves, achilles, lower back.

Heart Muscle Improvement

Sprint 8 Cardio can also significantly improve heart muscle efficiency in just a few months. Maria sent an e-mail with her heart rate graphed during Sprint 8. Her heart rate (HR) graphs show, over a six month period, the perfect example of one of the Sprint 8 goals -- to improve the efficiency of the heart muscle.

Maria's first heart rate measurement during Sprint 8 shows she is capable of working her heart muscle in the high-intensity zone (white on the graph below) at over 160 beats per minute (bpm).

The high-intensity marker decreases during aging. At age 20, high intensity is 175 bpm, age 40 it's 162 bpm, age 60 it's 149, and it can vary significantly between men and women.

During the first month of Sprint 8 (below), Maria was able to get her heart muscle up to 160 bpm, but the recovery of her heart muscle in between cardio sprints was very slow.

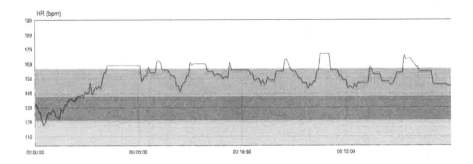

The conditioning of her heart muscle when she started Sprint 8 cardio was below where it should be as compared to her potential. Maria continued the Sprint 8 Cardio Protocol as a tool to significantly improve the condition of her heart muscle for three months. Notice her improvement on the second graph. Her heart muscle can now work at over 175 bpm during cardio sprints, and it is able to recover much faster in between the cardio sprints.

If you use a HRT monitor, this is exactly the performance improvement we should all be seeking. We want to see the heart muscle slowly and progressively get stronger so it can work hard and recover fast.

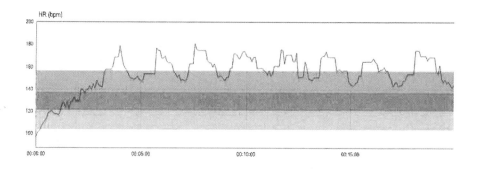

After six months of Sprint 8, Maria's heart muscle improved even more. Now her heart muscle can work extremely hard for the most strenuous anaerobic conditions. She can perform hard, anaerobic exercise at over 180 beats per minute (below). Also, notice how efficient her heart muscle recovers in between the cardio sprints.

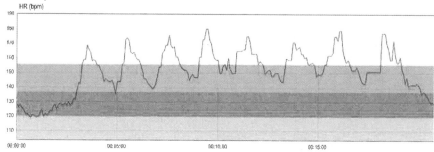

Maria's heart rate recovery after the last cardio sprint shows huge improvement. Her heart rate is down to close to the starting rate within two minutes of doing 8 reps of all-out, maximum-effort cardio sprints. Should you use a heart rate monitor, this is a perfect example of accomplishing one of the main goals of the Sprint 8 Protocol -- safely strengthening the heart muscle.

Sprint 8 not only strengthens the heart muscle, it also improves the circulatory system by creating new capillaries. The authors of *The Immortality Edge* describe what sprint cardio does for the body:

> *The repetitive form of exercise leads to an adaptive response. The **body begins to build new capillaries,** and it is better able to take in and deliver oxygen to the muscles. The muscles, in turn, develop a higher tolerance to the buildup of lactate, and the heart muscle is strengthened,* (Fossel, Blackburn, Woynarowski, (2011) *The Immortality Edge,* John Wiley p. 86-87).

Keeping Maximum Heart Rate Up During Aging

Your *maximum heart rate* is the fastest your heart will beat and pump blood throughout your entire body. I'm talking about your *real* maximum heart rate not some colors on the 220 minus your age HRT chart. Maintaining your maximum heart rate with a gentle decline during aging is desirable since this means your heart muscle is strong, and it's staying strong.

When your maximum heart rate declines too quickly during aging, this means the heart muscle is becoming weaker than it should, and it is becoming more susceptible to damage.

In a study at Ball State University by Drs. Ozemek and Kaminsky, their research clearly demonstrates men and women can successfully manage the decline of maximum heart rate during aging by continuing to maintain high levels of cardio fitness. In other words, use it or lose it. (Ozemek, C, & Kaminsky, L. (2016) *High Cardiorespiratory Fitness Levels Slow the Decline in Peak Heart Rate with Age.* Medicine & Science in Sports & Exercise: January 2016 - Volume 48 - Issue 1 - p 73–81).

Dr. Kaminsky and I were quoted in a *LA Times* article on HIIT 15 years ago, and I've been a fan of his research over the years.

For my Sprint 8 Challenge class, I teach a simple definition of cardio fitness that people can see on a heart monitor. Cardio fitness is *how hard you can work your heart muscle and how quickly it recovers* after a cardio sprint.

When comparing *maximum heart rate* performance side-by-side for six months, the benefits of Sprint 8 become clear. Maria started with a maximum heart rate average of 160 bpm (beats per minute). At age 50, she was slightly under her American Heart Association HRT calculation of *220 minus age* (220 - 50 = 170). She was 10 points below the standard calculation. This means her heart muscle was performing as an estimated 60-year old.

Initially, her heart muscle recovered during the 90-second active recovery 13 BPM (beats per minute), which means she didn't have much of a recovery between the cardio sprints. But her hard, consistent work of 20 minutes, three-days-a-week, had a major league pay off.

Heart Muscle Improvement

Beginning Sprint 8

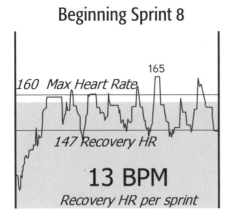

160 Max Heart Rate

165

147 Recovery HR

13 BPM
Recovery HR per sprint

Six Months Later

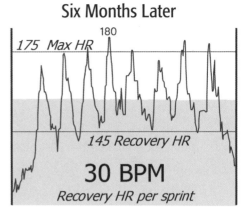

180

175 Max HR

145 Recovery HR

30 BPM
Recovery HR per sprint

Comparing the before and after measurements above, you can see significant improvement. Her heart muscle after six months of Sprint 8 is much stronger. Now she is able to do all eight reps of Sprint 8 at 175 bpm with one rep peaking at 180. Maria's 175 bpm *max heart rate* performance moves her to an estimated age of 45, which is a 15-year reversal in heart muscle performance based on the calculation of 220 minus age *maximum heart rate* prediction formula.

Remember, cardio fitness is *how hard you can work your heart muscle and how quickly it recovers.* Notice her outstanding improvement during recovery. Maria's heart rate now drops like a rock during the active recovery. It drops by 30 BPM (beats per minute) during the recovery. This is what you would expect to see in a much younger, very fit person.

Measuring her improvement in percentages, her heart muscle is 9.375 percent stronger, and she reversed the 220 minus age standard by 15 years. Her cardio fitness recovery has improved by 130 percent in six months.

Sprint-intensity training is shown to benefit overweight sedentary men. Researchers report:

> **Two weeks of Sprint-Intensity Training substantially improved a number of metabolic and vascular risk factors** in overweight/obese sedentary men, highlighting the potential for this to provide an alternative exercise model for the improvement of vascular and metabolic health in this population, (Whyte LJ, (2010 Oct), *Effect of 2 weeks of sprint interval training on health-related outcomes in sedentary overweight/obese men*. Metabolism. ;59(10):1421-8.).

Your Second Heart Muscle

Dr. Gabe Mirkin was one of the first physicians to widely publicize the fact that your muscles -- especially your leg muscles -- act as a second heart muscle. When you move your legs during exercise, even walking, the muscles contract synergistically to assist the heart muscle to pump blood throughout the body.

The body has roughly 60,000 miles of blood vessels and the heart beats approximately 100,000 times a day, pushing 2,250 gallons of blood throughout the body. When you walk or exercise your legs, it makes the large leg muscles contract and relax with every step. As shown in the following graphic, this process assists your heart muscle in pumping blood, and it means that your legs serve as a second heart muscle -- when you move them, of course.

If someone sits for hours and doesn't get up to walk, this means the heart muscle alone is doing all the work to pump blood through those 60,000 miles of blood vessels. Walking and standing frequently are very important and it will help to support the heart for basic aerobic activities.

If someone only walks and does long-slow cardio a few days a week, this training, while positive and burning a few calories, will only provide limited benefits because this only works the *slow-muscle fibe*r in the legs, and it only conditions the aerobic process of the heart muscle. Not only is it limiting, it is very inefficient for busy people.

Muscles (left) relaxed state
Muscles contracting (right) squeezing veins to pump blood

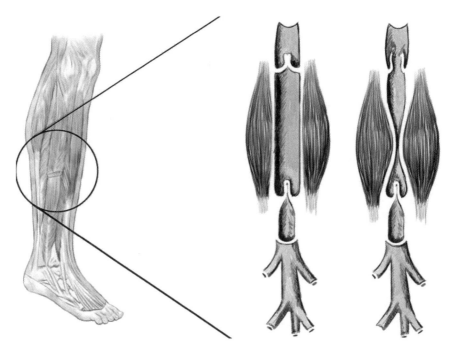

Graphic by Manoj Bhargav

The three-hour-a-week, Sprint 8 Challenge class that I coach has members doing the Sprint 8 Protocol at the beginning of the class. The fully mature program for this segment is 20 minutes. Never longer.

Sprint 8 cardio is followed by strength training for 20-30 minutes while growth hormone is circulating at high levels in the blood to achieve the synergistic effects of strength training immediately after giving yourself a huge natural injection of this powerful, muscle-building, body-fat reducing hormone -- growth hormone.

The class ends with the 10-Minute Stretching Routine discussed with photo illustrations in Chapter 6 of my book, *Ready, Set, Go! Fitness*.

Leg muscle development is so critically important that one full strength section in the Sprint 8 Challenge class is spent on comprehensively working all three *muscle-fiber types* in the legs. This strength training session is in addition to working the legs via Sprint 8 three-days-a-week.

Leg strength training is important. Your muscles, especially your leg muscles serve as your second heart. Dr. Mirkin explains;

> When you run, your heart pumps blood through your body, but it gets lots of help from your legs. When your leg muscles contract, they squeeze veins near them to push blood toward your heart. When your leg muscles relax, the veins near them fill with blood. **This alternate contracting and relaxing of your leg muscles serves as a second heart. When you sprint toward the finish line, your leg muscles increase their pumping of blood,** (Mirkin, G. *How to Strengthen Your Heart,* . *www.DrMirkin.com,* http://drmirkin.com/public/ezine080705.html. *Collapse After Exercise.* Mirkin, G. http://drmirkin.com/fitness/collapse.html*)

I highly recommend Dr. Mirkin's teaching and the information he and his wife Diana have posted on the Internet at *www.drMirkin.com*. If Dr. Mirkin says it, believe it.

The Sprint 8 Cardio Protocol clearly works your second heart muscle (your legs) by recruiting and strengthening all three *muscle fiber types; slow (Type I), fast (IIa)* and *super-fast (IIx)* muscle fiber.

Stand up at least once every half hour

Just as Sprint 8 takes you out of a calorie-counting world into a world of injecting growth hormone -- except it's all NATURAL -- prolonged sitting does just the opposite to negate the benefits of exercise.

Prolonged sitting takes you out of a calorie-counting world into a world of a defective, sluggish, inefficient body headed for weak bones and painful joints, insulin resistance and a body that is much older than its actual age.

While prolonged sitting is not as bad as crack for premature aging, it's just a slower pull of the trigger. Even if you exercise regularly, prolonged sitting is shown to be *associated with deleterious health outcomes regardless of physical activity,* (Aviroop Biswas, (2015, Jan. 20) *Sedentary Time and Its Association With Risk for Disease Incidence, Mortality, and Hospitalization in Adults: A Systematic Review and Meta-analysis.* Annuals of Internal Medicine, Vol 162, No. 2).

The World Health Organization (WHO) reports that lack of physical activity, which is far less intense than even low-intensity exercise, ranks #4 as causing premature deaths. The lack of physical activity kills an estimated 3.2 million people every year, and it is a key risk factor for cardiovascular diseases, cancer and diabetes. Globally, 1 in 4 adults and 8 out of 10 adolescents are insufficiently physically active.

The WHO clarifies physical activity is different than exercise. This is important because many people think physical activity is the same thing as exercise. They think *if you are active, you don't need to exercise.* This is not true. You need both. The World Health Organization reports;

> ***"Physical activity" should not be confused with "exercise,"*** *which is a subcategory of physical activity that is planned, structured, repetitive, and aims to improve or maintain one or more components of physical fitness,* (Physical Activity Fact sheet N°385, (2015, Jan.) World Health Organization).

You need both, physical activity AND vigorous intensity exercise. Even doing the demanding Sprint 8 for exercise, you should stand up for 5 minutes at least once every 30 minutes during the day and walk to and from lunch if you work at a desk.

In a major study at the Cooper Clinic, researchers investigated the relationship of *standing* and health measurements on over 7,000 patients ages 20-79. Researchers assessed the association between reported *standing time* and obesity, elevated waist circumference, body fat percentage, and metabolic syndrome.

The findings tell the story and set desirable goals for standing during the day. Those who would stand for 25 percent of the time or more had lower body fat percentage and better health measures. If you have a desk job and can average standing 15 minutes for every hour at work, you'll be on the mark. This will accomplish the daily physical activity goal, but keep in mind this does nothing toward the exercise goals.

The take home: Even if you do Sprint 8 three-times-a-week, and your work is sitting at a desk, you should *stand* up 25 percent of the time. Walking to and from parking, and walking to lunch count towards the 25 percent *standing* goal.

Bertha Campbell McClenny, 88, my mom, and my step-dad
Jacob McClenny, 96, Lt. Col., Air Force (Retired), do Sprint 8 on a
Matrix Fitness recumbent bike and stay active.

Case Study, Dr. Joe Mercola

I first met Dr. Mercola at a Greta Blackburn Fit Camp in Cancun, Mexico. Greta B is the creator of the original Fit Camp -- *www.fitcamp.com.* She brings in cutting-edge experts to provide the latest, hot-off-the-press health and longevity information and inspiration for her Fit Campers.

Well known physicians and health and fitness experts, Dr. Joe Mercola, and Dr. Dave Woynarowski, along with Dr. Bill Andrews were the marque names for the Cancun Fit Camp. Dr. Bill Andrews, an accomplished ultramarathon runner, is known internationally as the researcher responsible for discovering a telomerase activator derived from the *Astragalus Root* shown to have an impact on persevering telomere length.

I was invited by Greta to present on exercise-induced growth hormone and conduct some Sprint 8 workshops. Dr. Mercola came to the Sprint 8 presentation and did the Sprint 8 on the beach in Cancun, Mexico.

I didn't know that he went back home to do his own personal Sprint 8 research project until he called me with his impressive results. He posted them in several of his newsletters -- *www.mercola.com.* Dr. Mercola reports in his highly recommenced newsletter; in pertinent part:

Good News! High-Intensity Exercise May Limit Age-Related Telomere Shortening

In an exciting study published earlier this year, the researchers discovered that there's a direct association between reduced telomere shortening in your later years and high-intensity-type exercises—a perfect example of which is Sprint 8, which I'll review below. This is very exciting, as the prospect of being able to reduce telomere shortening—essentially stopping the cellular aging process that eventually kills you—is one of the most promising anti-aging strategies we know of to date.

Sprint 8 Exercises Effectively Increases Human Growth Hormone Production

The other exciting benefit of Sprint 8-style exercises is its ability to naturally increase your body's production of human growth hormone (HGH), which also plays a significant role in the aging process.

I recently ran an interview with fitness expert Phil Campbell, in which he further expounds on this important topic. Campbell is the author of the book "Ready Set Go," which explains how exercises that engage your super-fast muscle fibers can increase your HGH levels, and I had the great pleasure of meeting him at a fitness camp in Cancun, Mexico, earlier this year.

He taught me how to apply this high-intensity exercise technique, and it has literally transformed my physique and physical health the way no other form of exercise ever has!

It is called Sprint 8 because if you graph your heart rate, you will see that it peaks eight times during the workout. (A sample chart of my heart rate is below.) This technique is exponentially superior to regular cardio workouts and you're doing yourself a great disservice if you ignore it.

Heart Rate During Sprint 8

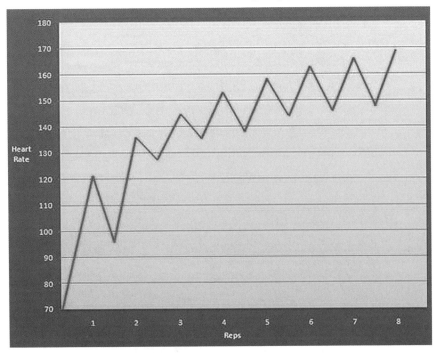

*I've been doing Sprint 8 exercises two or three times a week now since April of 2010, and so far I've **lost** over 17 pounds of fat and gained over 5 pounds of muscle.*

Body Fat % from 17.4% down to 9.1%

Melted 17.4 pounds of fat

Gained 5.4 pounds of muscle

Lost 3 3/16 inches off my waistline

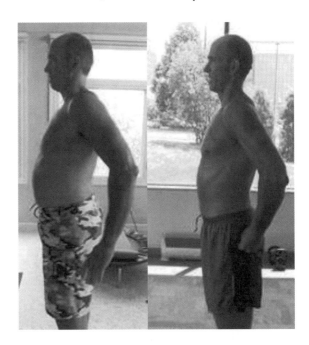

Why Sprint 8 Exercises are the Only Type of Exercise Capable of Increasing Your Levels of the "Fitness Hormone"

If you watch children (and most animals), you'll see perfect examples of natural movement. They don't run marathons, but rather sprint about at high speeds for short amounts of time, resting in between spurts. Essentially, they're performing "Sprint 8" exercises instinctively.

Your body was designed for this type of movement, and in response it produces growth hormone! HGH is what helps children grow, and in adulthood it helps you maintain optimal health and youthful vigor.

You can see the difference between Dr. Mercola's b*efore and after* Sprint 8 photos. There's more information at *www.mercola.com.* Dr. Mercola has videos posted demonstrating the intensity level it takes to achieve the exercise-induced growth hormone release benchmarks. Do an Internet search for *Sprint 8 Campbell Mercola* and the links should pop up.

There are many different ways to do Sprint 8

5

Benefits of Sprint 8

Attacks Cancer Cells

When you target the four Sprint 8 benchmarks to release exercise-induced growth hormone, there are many additional positive benefits.

Sprint-intensity cardio that achieves the adrenal response benchmark not only releases growth hormone, this also releases an enhanced immune system inside the body that is shown to target tumors in mice with a tumor-killing substance.

First, understand that mice don't jog. They don't know how. When mice enter a running wheel, they sprint on a self-propelled mice treadmill. Scientists have known that tumor-killing *NK immune cells* can attack tumors and reduce their size -- if they can find their way to the correct site in the body.

In 2016, researchers demonstrated in a major first-of-its-kind study that sprint-intensity cardio intense enough to release a surge of adrenaline into the body of mice, will also cause the body to move cancer-killing immune cells to the tumor sites implanted into the mice.

The exercise-induced adrenal response (one of the four Sprint 8 benchmarks) creates what the researchers call *IL-6 molecules*, which direct the tumor-killing immune cells to the site of the cancer to attack tumors.

The mice that were blocked from their running wheel and could not sprint, did *not* reduce tumor size. **The sprinting mice, reduced tumor size by 50 percent** because they received an adrenaline surge from their sprint cardio, (Line Pedersen. (February, 2016) *Voluntary Running Suppresses Tumor Growth through Epinephrine- and IL-6-Dependent NK Cell Mobilization and Redistribution.* Cell Metabolism).

The study spokesperson, Dr. Pernille Hojman, reported on these revolutionary findings:

> *That was actually a big surprise to us. As someone working in the field of exercise and oncology, one of the main questions that cancer patients always ask is: "How should I exercise? Can we do anything?"*
>
> *While it has previously been difficult to advise people about the intensity at which they should exercise, our data suggest that it might be beneficial to exercise at a somewhat high intensity in order to provoke a good adrenaline surge and hence recruitment of NK cells*, (Cell Press. (2016, February 16). *Running helps mice slow cancer growth. ScienceDaily*. Retrieved February 18, 2016 from www.sciencedaily.com releases/2016/02/160216142825.htm).

The white blood cells of the body's immune system produce *IL6* (short for Interleukin 6) and it regulates cell growth and plays an important role in immune response. This study, for all practical purposes, is telling us that when you use sprint-intensity cardio like the mice did, this exercise significantly helps the body attack tumors and reduces their size by 50 percent. Any way you cut it, this is very positive.

A physician friend said to me once, *you know what you are doing to people with Sprint 8, don't you. You are giving them a self-induced fever three-days-a-week.*

While fevers don't feel good, they are induced by the body for a reason. The hypothalamus (the same gland that tells the pituitary gland to release growth hormone) controls body temperature and when to fight infections, (Dinarello CA. (2004) *Infection, fever, and exogenous and endogenous pyrogens: some concepts have changed.* J Endotoxin Res.10(4):201-22).

The hypothalamus turns the heat up to help the body. Since the Sprint 8 also turns up the heat three-days-a-week, does this mean that the Sprint 8 Cardio Protocol is a tool used by the body to fire preemptive strikes at infections that enter the body from time-to-time? I don't have a definitive answer. But it is an interesting thought.

Beats Statin Drugs in Lowering Triglycerides

Eight weeks of Sprint 8 was compared with two top selling statin drugs, and the results were surprising.

While there is disagreement among medical professionals concerning the treatment for HDL (good) cholesterol and the LDL (bad) cholesterol, most seem to agree the circulating fat in the blood stream (triglycerides) is a major health issue that can be resolved. The 2012 study shows Sprint 8 is more effective than statin drugs in reducing *triglycerides* - though statins do better than exercise with LDL and HDL levels (Burt, D. (2012)*Targeting exercise-induced growth hormone release: A novel approach to fighting obesity by substantially increasing endogenous GH serum levels naturally*).

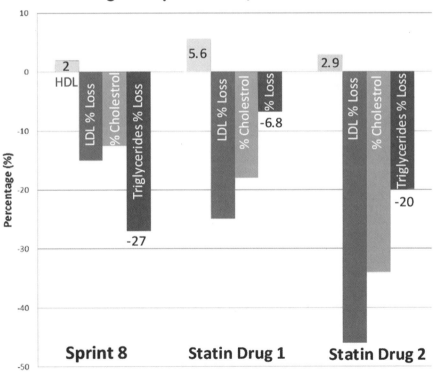

A Comparison of the Sprint 8 Trial with Statins drugs on Lipid Level %, Gains & Losses

High triglyceride levels are known to contribute to the thickening of artery walls, and this increases the risk of stroke, heart attack, heart disease, obesity and metabolic syndrome, (Mayo Clinic Foundation (August 15,2015), *Triglycerides: Why do they matter?*http://www.mayoclinic.org/triglycerides).

There may be a better way to control triglycerides and cholesterol, than simply to pop a pill -- especially after you see the nasty side effects of statins drugs. When you see what statins do to the body (below), consider talking with your physician about developing a new strategy.

The Mayo Clinic Foundation Newsletter highlights a discussion of the side effects of statin drugs:

> ***Muscle pain and damage*** *-- The most common statin side effect is muscle pain. You may feel this pain as a soreness, tiredness or weakness in your muscles. The pain can be a mild discomfort, or it can be severe enough to make your daily activities difficult. For example, you might find climbing stairs or walking to be uncomfortable or tiring. Statins can cause life-threatening muscle damage called Rhabdomyolysis, which can cause severe muscle pain, liver damage, kidney failure and death.* ***Side-effects*** *of liver damage, digestive problems, rash or flushing are reported with statin drugs.*
>
> ***Increased blood sugar or type 2 diabetes*** *-- It's possible your blood sugar (blood glucose) level may increase when you take a statin, which may lead to developing type 2 diabetes. The Food and Drug Administration (FDA) has issued a warning on statin labels regarding blood glucose levels and diabetes.*
>
> ***Neurological side effects*** *-- The FDA warns on statin labels that some people have developed memory loss or confusion while taking statins.*
>
> ***Statins may affect not only your liver's production of cholesterol but also several enzymes in muscle cells that are responsible for muscle growth. The effects of statins on these cells may be the cause of muscle aches,*** (Mayo Clinic Newsletter (April 24, 2013). *Statin side effects: Weigh the benefits and risks,* http://www.mayoclinic.org/statin-side-effects/art-20046013).

One out of four Americans over age 45 is taking a statin drug at the cost of $20 billion a year. People I know who take statin drugs have muscle and joint pain and frequently don't have the energy to exercise. Part of the muscle pain may be due to the fact statin drugs significantly lower coenzyme Q10 levels. Dr. Mercola's newsletter takes statins head on:

> **Statins deplete your body of coenzyme Q10** *(CoQ10), which accounts for many of their devastating results. Although it was proposed to add a black box warning to statins stating this, the U.S. Food and Drug Administration (FDA) decided against it in 2014.*
>
> **If you look at absolute risk, statin drugs benefit just 1 percent of the population.** *This means that out of 100 people treated with the drugs, one person will have one less heart attack. This doesn't sound so impressive, so statin supporters use a different statistic called relative risk, (Mercola, J. (February 10, 2016) 5 Great Reasons Why You Should Not to Take Statin Drugs.* Http://articles.mercola.com/sites/articles/archive/2016/02/10/5-reasons-why-you-should-not-take-statins.aspx).

For years it was thought the best treatment strategy for reducing the risk of heart disease and stroke was exercise along with statin drugs. Sounds reasonable until you look at the real life side-effects, and see the research that has been done.

When the combination of *exercise and statins* was studied, the results were shocking. Fitness levels of the research volunteers increased by 10 percent in response to exercise training alone. However, when statins were combined with exercise, fitness levels only improved by 1.5 percent.

Wow. What's going on here?

The New York Times Gretchen Reynolds answers this question:

> When the researchers looked microscopically at biopsied muscle tissue, they found notable differences in the levels of an enzyme related to the health of mitochondria, the energy-producing parts of a cell.
>
> Mitochondria generally increase in number and potency when someone exercises. **In the volunteers taking statins, enzyme levels related to mitochondrial health fell by about 4.5 percent** over the course

of the experiment. **The same levels increased by 13 percent in the group not taking the drug,** *(Gretchen Reynolds (May 22, 2013).* http://mobile.nytimes.com/blogs/well/2013/05/22/can-statins-curb-the-benefits-of-exercise).

The *New York Times* interviewed Dr. John P. Thyfault, professor of nutrition and exercise physiology at the University of Missouri where the study took place. He said, *In effect, the volunteers taking statins were not getting the same bang from their exercise buck as the other exercisers, (Mikus CR1, (2013 Apr 20).Simvastatin impairs exercise training adaptations.* J Am Coll Cardiol. ;62(8):709-14. Doi: 10.1016/j.jacc.2013.02.074.).

A major benefit of Sprint 8 is in cholesterol reduction without statin drugs. Statins are shown to limit the health improvement potential of exercise because these drugs appear to attack muscles in many people causing pain and problems for energy-producing mitochondria. This makes exercise less productive for those who take statins.

Investigating the impact of Sprint 8 on cholesterol reduction verses two top statin drugs, research spokesperson, Duane Burt reported:

The changes in serum lipid values were surprisingly unexpected, where the Sprint 8 protocol appears to mimic cholesterol-lowering medications. *This demands further investigation. As previously discussed, this free-living study required participants to adhere to their daily lives as usual, including no changes in diet or prescribed medications. A number of the Sprint 8 test subjects described after the brief 8 week trial* **they no longer required various medications they were previously prescribed, most of which were high blood pressure or cholesterol-reducing medications**.

While not all participants were at risk for CVDs, **cholesterol lowered 9.6 percent, LDL dropped 12.4 percent, triglycerides decreased 16.1 percent, while HDL increased 2.0 percent.**

The Sprint 8 program is a novel approach to potentially fighting the obesity epidemic and the many health and financial problems stemming from it. Beyond improving patient health, **the Sprint 8 program has the potential to relieve the burden placed on the health care** *industry by the innumerable diseases and disabilities derived from obesity and hyperlipidemia. Billions of dollars could be saved in health care expenses. As an alternative to the popular aerobic activities that require 30 minutes of exercise 5 days per week to be minimally effective and coupled with diets that depend on counting calories, the Sprint 8 proves to be time-efficient, at 20 minutes per bout, 3 bouts per week, for 8 weeks, totaling a mere 8 hours of exercise per 8 weeks, and requires no specific diet due to the significant amounts of GH the program yields. Building from this trial, as well as from future findings, an entire better way of life can be found for so many categorized as obese or not.*

Improves Brain Function

Lab reports of two individuals tested for the impact of Sprint 8 on dopamine release were simply amazing. This chemical doubled in one person, and it almost tripled in the other.

This is significant because low dopamine levels can lead to lack of motivation, fatigue, addictive behavior, mood swings and even memory loss. Our brain cells communicate with each other through chemicals called neurotransmitters. Dopamine is an important neurotransmitter that's a key contributor to our motivation, productivity, and focus. In other words, when you do Sprint 8 correctly, which significantly increases your dopamine levels, you should feel more motivated, productive and focused.

My take on the significant dopamine release from Sprint 8 means sprint cardio has several built-in motivational tools. Yes, Sprint 8 is hard. It's the hardest program you will ever do -- if you do it correctly. But you will see physical results in the mirror and smile when clothes are getting loose (without starving). You will feel the energy boost from the increase in ATP producing mitochondria. Additionally, the dopamine release may just be a built-in way to create extra motivation to continue exercising regularly.

Dopamine has a major role in controlling pleasure in the brain. It is released during Sprint 8 and during enjoyable situations, which stimulates people to seek out pleasurable things.

Many scientists believe dopamine has a major role in the euphoria experienced by runners called the *runners high*, (Boecker H. (1991). T*he runner's high: opioidergic mechanisms in the human brain. Cerebral cortex* (New York, N.Y.), 18 (11), 2523-31. PMID: 18296435)

Let me give you my highest recommendation for a book written by Dr. John Ratey, *SPARK, The New Revolutionary New Science of Exercise and the Brain.* (Little Brown and Company, 2008).

Dr. Ratey is an Associate Clinical Professor of Psychiatry at Harvard Medical School and is internationally recognized as one of the world's foremost authorities on the brain-fitness connection. Dr. Ratey writes:

> *We all know that exercise makes us feel better, but most of us have no idea why. We assume it's because we're burning off stress or reducing muscle tension or boosting endorphins, and we leave it at that. But the real reason we feel so good when we get our blood pumping is that it makes the brain function at its best, and in my view, this benefit of physical activity is far more important -- and fascinating -- than what it does for the body. **Building muscle and conditioning the heart and lungs are essentially side effects. I often tell my patients that the point of exercise is to build and condition the brain.***

To emphasize Dr. Ratey's point about brain fitness and clarity of thought, I often explain to people going through the eight week Sprint 8 Challenge that life is so busy and stressful that some people will take a year off from work to hike the Appalachian Trail in order to get back to nature and go down to the lowest levels of Maslow's Hierarchy, the physiological and safety level to clear their minds and appreciate life again.

I get this every time I do Sprint 8. I'm just glad to be alive, and I'm so glad that the 20-minute workout is over. I can tell you this, life is wonderful and sweet after the last cardio sprint. It's euphoric from a feeling of accomplishment, and the dopamine release definitely makes everyone happy after rep 8 is completed. Sprint 8 clearly has an anti-depressive effect, at least, once it's over.

Dr. David J. Linden, professor in the Department of Neuroscience at the Johns Hopkins University School of Medicine reports on the benefits of exercise on brain function:

> *Voluntary exercise is also associated with long-term improvements in mental function and is the single best thing one can do to slow the cognitive decline that accompanies normal aging.* ***Exercise has a dramatic anti-depressive effect****. It blunts the brain's response to physical and emotional stress.* ***A regular exercise program produces a large number of changes in the brain, including the new growth and branching of small blood vessels*** *and increases in the geometric complexity of some neuronal dendrite,* (Linden, D. *Exercise, pleasure and the brain Understanding the biology of "runner's high,* Psychology Today, Apr 21, 2011).

In another study on sprinting mice on a running wheel, researchers show the sprinting mice actually create new brain cells with this form of exercise.

This is called *exercise-induced neurogenesis,* which means *birth of new brain cells*. Before these recent studies, it was thought neurogenesis happened during pre-natal development. Now those sprinting mice have demonstrated it can happen during the aging process -- only if you achieve the adrenal response with sprint-cardio that releases growth hormone, (Llorens-Martin, (2009) *Mechanisms mediating brain plasticity: IGF1 and adult hippocampal neurogenesis.* The Neuroscientist, 15, 134-148).

It's clear, Sprint 8 does many great things for your body, but as Dr. Ratey explains it -- exercise may be better for your mind. When I did my first book, *Ready, Set, Go, Fitness,* I learned one of the top selling markets was in Massachusetts -- in Dr. Ratey's neck-of-the-woods. This was due to Dr. Ratey recommending the book to his friends and patients.

When Dr. Ratey wrote *SPARK, The New Revolutionary New Science of Exercise and the Brain,* he sent an autographed copy to me with the inscription *Keep up the great and important work,* I was absolutely thrilled.

This was a personal dopamine-releasing moment worth remembering because Dr. Ratey is, in my opinion, the foremost expert in the world on brain-fitness. In his book he discusses how growth hormone and other hormones being released during exercise impact the body and the brain in many positive ways.

In a related study researchers show increasing growth hormone will help improve the ability to learn, reason, memorize, and focus. They report:

> *Emerging data indicate that growth hormone therapy could have a role in improving cognitive function. GH replacement therapy in experimental animals and human patients counteracts the dysfunction of many behaviors related to the central nervous system.* (Hallberg M. (2013 Jun 9) *Growth hormone and cognitive function. N*at Rev Endocrinol.(6):357-65. doi: 10.1038/nrendo.2013.78).

While these researchers studying the impact of injecting growth hormone, we have seen throughout this book the natural way to increase growth hormone generally achieves the same or better benefits, and exercise is as natural as you can get.

In *SPARK,* Dr. Ratey reports on a landmark study that compares the SSRI drug, sertraline (Zoloft) against exercise three-days-a-week. The lead researcher, Dr. Blumenthal concluded that **exercise was as effective as medication typically given for depression**.

Dr. Ratey adds, *This is the study I photocopy for patients who are skeptical of the idea that exercise changes their brain chemistry enough to help their depression*, (Ratey, *SPARK.* p. 122).

Growth Hormone is the body's master craftsman, burning belly fat, layering on muscle fiber, and pumping up brain volume. Researchers believe It can reverse the loss of brain volume that occurs as you age.

Dr. John Ratey, (2008). *SPARK, The New Revolutionary New Science of Exercise and the Brain.* p. 256 (Little Brown).

6

Want More Energy?

Why have coffee shops exploded in growth in recent years? I was walking across an intersection the other day and noticed there seemed to be a coffee shop on every corner. I don't think the growth of coffee shops is due to people *wanting* to pay $5 for a cup of coffee. I believe it's because people *want more energy*. People want to be alert. People want to feel good. Would you like more energy to do things in your life? If so, this chapter is for you.

Want more energy, here's how

Energy in the body is produced at the cellular level in our mitochondria. Mitochondria are tiny and can only be seen with a very powerful microscope. Although small, their function in the body is huge.

Mitochondria are frequently described as nuclear power plants of the cells. This is the place inside your muscle cells where carbohydrate, fat, and protein are broken down in the presence of oxygen to create *energy*. Mitochondria essentially takes what we eat and the oxygen we breathe to make a chemical substance called ATP *(Adenosine Triphosphate)*, which is energy in the body.

Mitochondria are located in almost every cell type in the body. They are distributed throughout your body with the main purpose of generating energy for life's activities.

The formula is simple. If you want more energy, you need more mitochondria. The good news is you don't have to have some genetic alteration overseas to get more mitochondria. In fact, you can get more for free.

Sprint 8 will significantly increase the amount of mitochondria in your muscle cells in a short time frame. I frequently explain to people their endurance capacity will double in two weeks of starting Sprint 8. And that's not doing all eight reps.

It generally takes several weeks to build up to eight reps. It's simply starting with two reps during the first workout and slowly building to eight reps over time. This method will significantly increase the number of mitochondria in your muscle cells, and you will physically feel the extra energy. This isn't a placebo. It's real. Just try it and you will see. You should begin feeling your energy levels increase within a few Sprint 8 workouts.

Mitochondria are the cell's energy factory that makes ATP to fuel all of life's activities

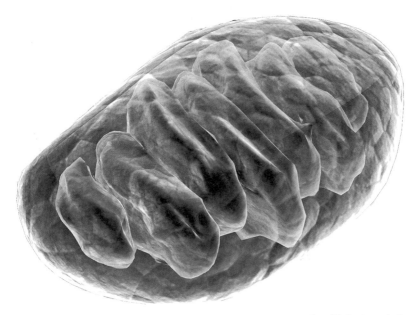

Graphic by Manoj Bhargav

A single Mitochondrion shown above. This is the source of energy in the body.

Studying mitochondria can reveal the effectiveness of different forms of exercise, and mitochondria studies clearly show HIIT gets the best results.

I consider Dr. John Holloszy the Father of HIIT. He is a professor at Washington University in St. Louis and was the first to do major work studying the process now called mitochondrial biogenesis. Dr. Holloszy demonstrated in the 1960s exercise increases mitochondria in the muscle cells, (Holloszy, J. (1967) *Effects of Exercise on Mitochondrial Oxygen Uptake and Respiratory Enzyme Activity in Skeletal Muscle,* Biological Chemistry, vol. 242(9), pp. 2278-2282).

Over the years, research building on Dr. Holloszy's pioneering work shows that *fast-twitch muscle* training at 100% intensity will roughly triple mitochondria output in 8 weeks. Dr. Gary Dudley with the State University of New York at Syracuse expanded on Dr. Holloszy's research in the 1980s. These researchers show high-intensity exercise is clearly more productive.

At the time Holloszy and Dudley performed their work in the field, the world was into long-slow aerobic training. These researchers were clearly swimming up stream. Many of the high-intensity programs we see today are built on the shoulders of their pioneering research. These researchers didn't create *Body by Celebrity* exercise programs. They were the leaders in researching and teaching high intensity is the key to exercise productivity.

To sum up Dr. Dudley's perspective on exercise intensity as it impacts mitochondria, he wrote:

> *To bring about the greatest adaptive response in mitochondria, the length of daily exercise becomes less as the intensity of the exercise is increased,* (Dudley G. J. (1982) Influence of exercise intensity and duration on biochemical adaptations in skeletal muscle. Appl. Physiol 53, 844 850).

The takeaway is sprint-intensity training has a much more profound effect on your body than any other form of exercise. Sprint 8 will increase the number of mitochondria and their efficiency to give you more energy. Researchers report:

> *High-intensity short-duration interval training stimulates functional and metabolic adaptation in skeletal muscle.* **After only 2 weeks HIT significantly increased mitochondrial function,** (Vincent G. (2015 Feb.) *Changes in mitochondrial function and mitochondria associated protein expression in response to 2-weeks of high intensity interval training.* Front Physiol. 24;6:51).

While there are skeptics who argue there is very little research to justify the case for taking vitamin supplements. When it comes to mitochondria, however, researchers conclude; *A multivitamin-mineral supplement is one low-cost way to ensure intake of the Recommended Dietary Allowance of micro nutrients throughout life, (Ames, B. N. (2006). Low micronutrient intake may accelerate the degenerative diseases of aging through allocation of scarce micro nutrients by triage.* Proc Natl Acad Sci U S A 103, 17589-17594).

In an interview with mitochondria researcher, George Schreiner Jr., MD, PhD, he explained why the original recommendation in *Ready, Set, GO! Fitness* of 2 grams of L-glutamine to help facilitate the release of exercise-induced growth hormone prior to doing Sprint 8 was also positive for mitochondria growth -- since *L-glutamine is fuel for mitochondria.* I stand by the recommendation of 2 grams of L-glutamine 30-minutes to one-hour before doing Sprint 8.

Based on Ames research report on the previous page, *Low micronutrient intake may accelerate the degenerative diseases of aging*, adding a daily *multivitamin-mineral* supplement is needed and positive.

If you want more *energy*, then you'll want more mitochondria. A typical animal muscle cell will have approximately 1,000 to 2,000 mitochondria. If we did a biopsy of the muscle in your legs *before* and *after* an eight-week Sprint 8 study, the *after* biopsy should reveal the numerical count increased by at least double, if not greater. If we checked the output of your mitochondria with a Cytochrome C test, the *after* picture would also show your mitochondria to be essentially three times more productive.

From the perspective of researching the impact of sprint-intensity on endurance capacity (which is like checking the math for the mitochondria equation), Gibala's research demonstrates in a landmark study that people can double their endurance capacity in two weeks with repeated 30-second cycling cardio sprints.

> *We conclude that short **sprint interval training** (approximately 15 minutes of intense exercise **over 2 weeks**) increased muscle oxidative potential and **doubled endurance capacity** during intense aerobic cycling in recreationally active individuals,* (Burgomaster K, Gibala, M. (2005, Jun). *Six sessions of sprint interval training increases muscle oxidative potential and cycle endurance capacity in humans.* J Appl Physiol)

The research picture is clear. You should expect to experience more *energy* within two weeks of starting the Sprint 8 Cardio Protocol.

The New York Times ran a major story by Gretchen Reynolds titled *The Best Exercise for Aging Muscles,* which discusses a major new study on how different forms of exercise compare in results. Researchers compared HIIT, strength training, and a combination of strength training and a lower-intensity interval training. Gretchen Reynolds reported:

*There were some unsurprising differences: The gains in muscle mass and strength were greater for those who exercised only with weights, while interval training had the strongest influence on endurance. But more unexpected results were found in the biopsied muscle cells. Among the younger subjects who went through **interval training, the activity levels had changed in 274 genes, compared with 170 genes for those who exercised more moderately and 74 for the weight lifters.** Among the older cohort, almost 400 genes were working differently now, compared with 33 for the weight lifters and only 19 for the moderate exercisers.*

The research is very clear. The highest-intensity exercise (that I call *sprint-intensity* so people understand the level of intensity it takes to get the job done) is the most productive form of exercise. This doesn't mean to stop doing strength training. This study doesn't say that. You need both, Sprint 8 Cardio and strength training during the week. My first book, *Ready Set, GO! Synergy Fitness for Time-Crunched Adults* has 380 pages and hundreds of demonstration photos showing how to add strength training to your weekly training plan.

The E-Lift technique in Ready, Set, Go Chapters 9 and 10 is to strength training what Sprint 8 is to cardio. E-Lift is a simple technique to recruit fast-muscle fiber so you work all three muscle-fiber types for superior results while saving time. E-Lifts are used on push and press strength exercises in the Sprint 8 Challenge Class.

Only working slow muscle fiber during strength training means that in order to get progressive overload for continued results, you will have to keep going longer and longer and heavier and heavier. E-Lift technique shows you how to use *velocity of movement* to force the brain to recruit all three muscle-fiber types so you get better results and save time.

In a nutshell, use the E-Lift technique during push and press exercises. When you are pushing the resistance away from the body, the E-Lift technique works great. Some call this a *pause rep*, which is a cousin of the E-Lift, but not the same. Pause reps emphasize the pause (and you do want to pause in a static-still position), but pause reps don't emphasize the mission critical aspect of the E-Lift technique -- the explosive, without momentum, fast-as-you-can, velocity push away-from-the-body, max-effort repetition during every rep of the set.

It looks like a pause rep, but it's significantly more intense because you are recruiting a lot more muscle fiber to propel the movement. For example, people who can do 100 push-ups will typically only be able to do 19 to 23 E-Lift technique push-ups before failing. Don't believe me? Put it to the test right now. If you don't pause, don't count the rep.

You have to fully stop and embellish the static-still pause in the lower position. Now, without momentum, explode up fast as possible. Don't just drop back down into the pause position -- Control it Lower your body down slow and controlled to the lower position and get static still before the following rep.

You may notice (as many people do) that your brain takes over and it doesn't let you stop and pause on some reps. This is your brain trying to go back to slow fiber propelling the exercise. Don't count the non-stop reps. Only count the reps where you come to a complete stop, pause, and without momentum, explode up fast-as-you-can. This is an E-Lift.

E-Lifting technique is not necessarily opposite of the *slow reps* strength training strategy. Here's why. Performing a *slow rep* or a *super-slow rep,* you are increasing intensity by slowing down the velocity of movement. This can be positive for beginners and people doing rehab and prehab because it creates microtrauma in the muscles being worked while using less weight.

During strength training, you get intensity from the amount of resistance, number of sets / reps and the *velocity of the movement.* While slow reps can be very positive and should be a tool in every trainer's arsenal, there is one issue that limits the productivity of slow reps. The slow tempo does increase intensity with less weight, but it does not recruit fast-muscle fiber. Thinking that slow reps recruits all three fiber types is the same thinking that sprinters need to train longer and slower to get faster. Muscles don't work like this. There are three muscle-fiber types and all three need to be strengthened by being recruited and worked.

The great news is *slow reps* and *E-Lift*s can be combined to accomplish goals of both forms of strength training, as both techniques increase intensity via the velocity of movement. You can use the slow and controlled tempo lowering the weight, pause in a static-still position, and without momentum, explode out to recruit all three muscle-fiber types. How to know it this is working? You may find yourself sweating on a push up or a chest press where you have never sweated before. This is because your heart muscle and lungs are having to work harder to oxygenate a lot more muscle fiber than before.

7

Long Telomeres for Health & Longevity

The Sprint 8 Cardio Protocol can be used by anyone at any age. Just because we quit using our *fast-muscle fiber* a few years ago, those cells haven't disappeared. They are just small and wimpy BECAUSE THEY DON'T GET USED. Begin recruiting both types of *fast-muscle fiber,* and you'll do great things to preserve the length of your telomeres. Here's why your telomere length is so important.

When looking at longevity, it's important to understand new discoveries concerning your telomeres. What they are and what they do. Most importantly, it's important to know how you can keep your telomeres healthy.

We saw in the Chapter *Want More Energy?*, the significant impact that cellular-sized mitochondria has on the body. In this chapter, we will look at the impact telomeres have on the body.

As impressive as the results are for sprint-intensity cardio on cellular-level mitochondria, Sprint 8 is also great for your chromosomes, specifically, the ends of your chromosomes, which are called **telomeres.** Telomeres make it possible for our cells to divide correctly, and they may hold the key to living longer and cancer. You can only see telomeres under a very powerful microscope.

The following graphic shows what chromosomes look like. The two dots at the ends of the chromosomes are telomeres.

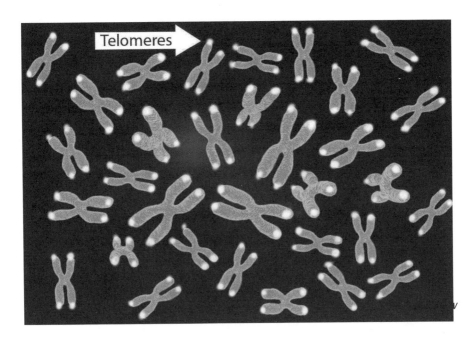

Zooming in on chromosomes for a closer look, telomeres look like two tails located on both ends of your chromosome strains. Telomeres deter the degradation of your genes. In other words, they protect the cells from aging too quickly. They are somewhat like the caps on the end of shoelaces protecting them from fraying.

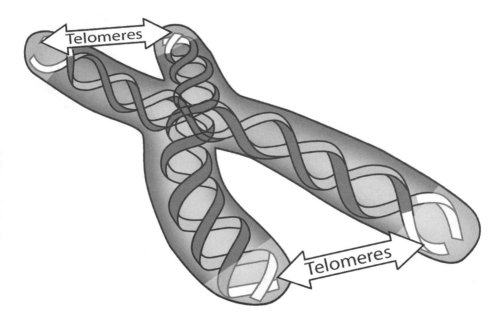

Researchers show telomeres appear to measure biological aging (as opposed to chronological aging). Telomeres are the protective caps on the ends of chromosomes that affect how fast your cells age. They are combinations of DNA and protein that protect the ends of chromosomes and help them remain stable. As telomere length becomes shorter, the structural integrity weakens, the cells age and die quicker.

Shorter telomeres are associated with a broad range of aging-related diseases, including many forms of cancer, stroke, vascular dementia, cardiovascular disease, obesity, osteoporosis and diabetes.

The length of telomeres indicates what condition the body is in. Long telomeres are associated with health and longevity. Conversely, short telomeres points to premature aging. They are in effect *cellular timekeepers* -- and they are a more accurate gauge than your biological age.

Telomeres are tied in to natural growth hormone release. Albert Einstein College of Medicine's study of centenarians concluded telomere length is associated with exceptional longevity; telomere length is modulated by the Insulin-like Growth Factor (IGF, or Growth Hormone) system, and telomere-shortening and decline in IGF levels are features of aging.

The key here is making sure your telomeres are long, stay long, or prevent them from shortening further if you have already started sliding downhill in the biological age department.

So how do you ensure your telomeres are long? Can you do something to help them? Recent research on telomeres shows telomere length *is preserved in healthy older adults who perform vigorous aerobic exercise.*

To be specific, telomere length is positively related to *maximal aerobic exercise capacity.* Researchers note this may represent *a novel molecular mechanism underlying the anti-aging effects of maintaining high aerobic fitness.*

Vigorous, hard and fast cardio exercise releases growth hormone -- and in turn, positively affects telomere length. Sprint 8 can be a valuable tool to improve health at the cellular level. It can be a life-long weapon to fight the symptoms of aging at the cellular level.

Research on telomeres absolutely validates the use of Sprint 8 training for maintaining top level fitness and fighting the symptoms of aging. On the flip side, failure to workout like this can cause negative measures for your telomeres.

The American Heart Association reports weight gain is correlated with faster telomere shortening. In a study conducted by University of California at San Francisco, lead author Dr. Dean Ornish reported:

> *Our genes, and our telomeres, are not necessarily our fate. So often people think 'Oh, I have bad genes, there's nothing I can do about it. But these findings indicate that telomeres may lengthen to the degree that people change how they live. Research indicates that* **longer telomeres are associated with fewer illnesses and longer life***, (Ornish, (2015, Sept. 16)* Lifestyle Changes May Lengthen Telomeres, A Measure of Cell Aging. The Lancet Oncology).

In this five-year study, the researchers followed 35 men with localized, early-stage prostate cancer to explore the relationship between comprehensive lifestyle changes and telomere length and telomerase activity.

One group changed their lifestyle to include a healthy diet and regular exercise, and their telomere length was compared to those who didn't make the same lifestyle changes. The group that made the lifestyle changes experienced an increase in telomere length of approximately 10 percent. The more people changed their behavior by adhering to the recommended lifestyle program, the more dramatic their improvements in telomere length.

By contrast, the men in the control group who were not asked to alter their lifestyle had shorter telomeres, nearly 3 percent shorter when the five-year study ended. Telomere length decreases over time. It's very clear in the research, if someone wants to beat the symptoms of aging, it can be done naturally.

At this point, let me recommend a must-read book on telomeres. *The Immortality Edge* by Michael Fossel, M.D., PhD, Greta Blackburn and Dave Woynaroski, MD, CPT, is the definitive work on telomeres with real life application on how to slow the shortening of telomeres during aging. I personally know all three authors, and let me tell you, they know their stuff. Others have written about telomere science, but these authors put the science in a nutshell and they provide real life application that is affordable for all. The authors report:

> *Even more impressive, from our point of view, is some recent research in Italy that found that high levels of HGH correlate with*

longer telomere. Measurements for both were taken from 476 healthy people (both men and women) between the ages of 16 and 104, and after the effect of age was factored in, it was determined **high HGH levels accounted for a 10 percent increase in telomere length,** *(*Woynarowski, D. (2001) *The Immortality Edge, Realize the Secrets of Your Telomeres,* Wiley p.88).

NOTE: Author Dr. Dave Woynarowski has an excellent newsletter at *www.drdavesbest.com.*

The authors also discussed the necessity of working *fast-muscle fiber* during exercise. They report:

> *Fast-twitch explosive fibers burn primarily sugar and store short-term energy sources such as creatine. They burn almost no fat (although the work they do is a major stimulus for burning fat in the recovery phase). They kick in when you need explosive, fast, or very powerful, rapid reactions. Our Paleolithic Ancestors had to run to save their lives from saber-toothed tigers. Today, any New Yorker will tell you that it doesn't hurt to be able to race across a crosswalk in rush-hour traffic,* *(The Immortality Edge, p.85).*

Telomeres are absolutely necessary for life. Telomeres allow cells to divide without losing genes. Cell division is necessary for life, but if we didn't have telomeres to protect our genes that are housed inside the main part of the chromosome, the ends could fuse together and corrupt the cell's genetic code. Corrupting this code would not be positive. This leads genes to malfunction, possibly sparking a cancerous growth.

According to Dr. Tomislav Meštrovi , MD, PhD, **A majority of human cancers exhibit critically short telomeres,** *suggesting that tumors can arise from genetically unstable cells with dysfunctional telomeres,* (*Telomeres and Cancer, (2015, Nov 19), Mestrovi, T, News-Medical,* http://www.news-medical.net/life-sciences/Telomeres-and-Cancer.aspx)

Any way you cut it, keeping your telomeres long naturally with exercise is clearly positive in fighting the symptoms of aging. There are also indications sprint-intensity cardio can fight cancer before it becomes embedded.

Vitamin D Associated with
Longer Telomeres & Preventing Cancer

Vitamin D is a vitamin (sold as Vitamin D³ supplements), and it is also classified as a hormone because it controls important functions in the body; like helping the body to use calcium. In its hormone role, Vitamin D is shown to be very important in muscle function, modulation of cell growth, immune function, and reduction of inflammation.

Vitamin D is shown to be too low for 57 percent of the population. Researchers report:

> *Adequate vitamin D is also important for **proper muscle functioning** ... it may help **prevent** type 1 diabetes, hypertension, and **many common cancers.** Vitamin D inadequacy has been reported in approximately 36% of otherwise healthy young adults and up to 57% of general medicine inpatients in the United States,* (Holick, M. F. (2006). High prevalence of vitamin D inadequacy and implications for health. Mayo Clinic proceedings. Mayo Clinic 81, 353-373).

Researchers investigating the role of Vitamin D and telomere length, have learned people who have higher Vitamin D levels from supplements also have longer telomeres:

> *Our findings suggest higher Vitamin D concentrations, which are **easily modifiable through nutritional supplementation**, are associated with longer LTL, (Telomere Length) which **underscores the potentially beneficial effects of this hormone on aging and age-related diseases**,* (Richards, JB. (2007). Higher serum vitamin D concentrations are associated with longer leukocyte telomere length in women. The American Journal of Clinical Nutrition, 86(5):1420-1425).

Researchers also show that shorter telomere length and illnesses may be directly related to low levels of Vitamin D:

> **Because shorter telomere length has been associated with many chronic illnesses that Vitamin D has been shown to protect against**, *it is possible that a mechanism of Vitamin D's protection is through the maintenance of telomere integrity*, (Liu, J. J. (2013) *Plasma vitamin D biomarkers and leukocyte telomere length.* American journal of epidemiology 177, 1411-1417).

These studies clearly show Vitamin D^3 supplements are needed and necessary for good health because it helps to preserve the length of our telomeres. What we don't know is how much Vitamin D^3 supplement we need every day, and how much is too much.

The *too much* question is the easy one. The Vitamin D Council reports if you take more than 10,000 to 40,000 Units per day, *everyday* for 3 months this could lead to Vitamin D toxicity, (http://www.vitamindcouncil.org/about-vitamin-d/am-i-getting-too-much-vitamin-d/). Since most Vitamin D^3 supplements are sold as 1000 IUs (International Units) per capsule, this is 10 to 40 pills a day. That's a lot of pills to swallow.

Now for the *how much* question. There is a range with four main levels of recommendations based on scientific research, publications, traditional use, and expert opinion. The new recommended daily allowance (RDA) for Vitamin D^3 is:

Infants age 0 to 6 months: adequate intake, 400 IU/day; maximum safe upper level of intake, 1,000 IU/day

Infants age 6 to 12 months: adequate intake, 400 IU/day; maximum safe upper level of intake, 1,500 IU/day

Age 1-3 years: adequate intake, 600 IU/day; maximum safe upper level of intake, 2,500 IU/day

Age 4-8 years: adequate intake, 600 IU/day; maximum safe upper level of intake, 3,000 IU/day

Age 9-70: adequate intake, 600 IU/day; maximum safe upper level of intake, 4,000 IU/day

Age 71+ years: adequate intake, 800 IU/day; maximum safe upper level of intake, 4,000 IU/day,

The median recommendation comes from Dr. Michael Holick, PhD, professor of medicine at Boston University Medical Center. He recommends a dose of *1,000 IU a day of Vitamin D³ for both infants and adults -- unless they're getting plenty of safe sun exposure.*

The Vitamin D Council recommends *2,000 IU of Vitamin D daily -- more if they get little or no sun exposure,* (DeNoon, Daniel. (2010). http://www.webmd.com/osteoporosis/features/the-truth-about-vitamin-d-how-much-vitamin-d-do-you-need).

The upper range comes from the newsletter of a trusted physician friend who takes on tough health issues publicly head on and reports the facts without the fluff, Dr. Joe Mercola. I want to give Dr. Mercola's natural health newsletter the highest and best rating I can give. If you are interested in health information, you'll want to subscribe for free at *www.mercola.com.*

Dr. Mercola's newsletter reported on the findings from a medical conference about Vitamin D, and how it can be used to prevent breast cancer, colon cancer, high-blood pressure and diabetes. It has also been shown to reduce falls in the elderly.

The medical experts estimated *25 to 50 percent of any healthcare budget could be saved with adequate Vitamin D serum levels.* They also formulated new Vitamin D³ daily dose recommendations that are higher than the others:

Below 5   *35 IU/day per pound*
Age 5 - 10 *2,500 IU/day*
Adults   *4,000-8,000 IU/day*
Pregnant   *5,000-10,000 IU/day*

Since there are several ranges of Vitamin D³ recommendations available, the *Mercola.com* newsletter adds an important warning that I'd like to include in this book:

*WARNING: There is no way to know if the above recommendations are correct. **The ONLY way to know is to test your blood.** You might need four to five times the amount recommended above. Ideally, your blood level of 25(OH)D should be 60ng/ml.* (Mercola, J. (2016) http://articles.mercola.com/sites/articles/archive/2009/10/10/vitamin-d-experts-reveal-the-truth.aspx).

You can get a Vitamin D test from your physician, or you can order an online test kit from the Vitamin D Council ($50) at *www.vitamindcouncil.org/testkit/*.

It's clear that we all need Vitamin D supplements. I wish I could report all the experts agree on a simple daily recommended dose for Vitamin D. I can't. Vitamin D actually has a *U-shaped risk* curve (an upside down bell-shaped curve), reports Dr. Tuohimaa, which means too little vitamin D is bad, and too much Vitamin D is also bad, *(Tuohimaa, P. (2009). Vitamin D and aging.* The Journal of steroid biochemistry and molecular biology 114, 78-840.

Dr. Rhonda Patrick calls the U-shaped risk, the Vitamin D *Sweet Spot.* She has posted a fact-filled discussion, *The "Vitamin D Sweet Spot" and Its Relationship To Aging* at *http://blog.wellnessfx.com/2013/08/14/the-vitamin-d-sweet-spot-and-its-relationship-to-aging/.* Dr. Rhonda Patrick is a PhD in Biomedical Science and an expert in nutrition, metabolism, and aging, *(www.foundmyfitness.com).*

Here is the *take home* on Vitamin D. People who have the highest levels of Vitamin D, have the longest lifespan. People with the lowest levels of Vitamin D, have the shortest lifespan.

Magic Bullet for Telomere Health

Here is even more proof about the positive impact of sprint-intensity cardio on telomere length. Researchers at the University of Colorado report in the study, *Telomere length is preserved with aging in endurance exercise-trained adults and related to maximal aerobic capacity* the following conclusion:

> Our results indicate **Telomere length is preserved in healthy older adults who perform vigorous aerobic exercise and is positively related to maximal aerobic exercise capacity**. *This may represent a novel molecular mechanism underlying the "anti-aging" effects of maintaining high aerobic fitness,* (Larocca T.J., (2010 Feb) Department of Integrative Physiology, University of Colorado, Boulder. Mech Ageing Dev. ;131(2):165-7).

I hope you noticed the researchers statement about telomere length being ***positively related to maximal aerobic exercise*** because that's what Sprint 8 is, and that's what Sprint 8 is all about.

Sprint 8 Can Improve Metabolic Syndrome

Metabolic Syndrome is a disorder of the metabolism where the body makes someone fat in an abnormally fast way. In other words, Metabolic Syndrome makes the body become a body fat making machine. There is a way to fight back.

An additional key benefit to Sprint 8 training is it is one of the few exercise tools that can effectively fight Metabolic Syndrome. As a person gets older, the possibility of falling into the Metabolic Syndrome diagnosis increases substantially with age and waist line. The NIH: National Institute of Diabetes and Digestive and Kidney Diseases points out Metabolic Syndrome is a group of conditions that put you at risk for heart disease and diabetes. These conditions are:

- *High blood pressure*
- *High blood sugar levels*
- *High levels of triglycerides, circulating fat in your blood stream*
- *Low levels of HDL (good cholesterol) in your blood*
- *Too much body fat around the waist*

Insulin resistance plays the leading role in the cause of metabolic disease. Insulin is a hormone your body produces to help turn sugar from food into energy for your body. If you are insulin resistant, too much sugar builds up in your blood, setting the stage for disease.

Metabolic Syndrome is a health hazard that is affecting more and more people in the general population. Someone doesn't have to be obese to experience Metabolic Syndrome. Simply being medically overweight can do it too.

Researchers make it clear how to fight back -- strengthen and build muscle while reducing body fat.:

> *Muscular strength and cardiorespiratory fitness have independent and joint inverse associations with metabolic syndrome prevalence,* (Jurca R, (2004 Aug) *Associations of muscle strength and fitness with metabolic syndrome in men.* Med Sci Sports Exerc).

Metabolic Syndrome Sliding Scale

Lean & mean *Normal glucose metabolism*	During aging **Losing muscle gaining body fat** *»»» Increasing resistance to insulin »»»*	Pre-Diabetes *Problems with glucose*	Diabetes *Body can't effectively clear glucose*

The Metabolic Syndrome Sliding Scale shows many start out *Lean & mean* in their youth, but *during the aging process* begin to increase body fat and lose muscle. If we are **not** careful to fight this process, the body reaches the *pre-diabetic* and *diabetes* stages of poor glucose (sugar) processing.

The aging process isn't the key cause of Metabolic Syndrome. Researchers are clear it's the muscle to body fat composition that is directly related to people with climbing insulin resistance that occurs during aging. If we don't maintain muscle and keep body fat from slowly creeping up, we develop Metabolic Syndrome.

This is another reason we all should strengthen and build muscle as we age. Building muscle isn't just for athletes to improve performance, and it isn't just a *guy thing*. Building muscle and controlling body fat is extremely important for *everyone*, men and women, young and old. This is especially important for men, and maybe more important for women during aging.

Exercise is a powerful tool in overcoming Metabolic Syndrome during aging so the body can effectively manage glucose (sugar) along the way. When you build strength and muscle in your body, you tip the scale and begin moving in the opposite direction *away* from Metabolic Syndrome and back towards the *Lean & mean* metabolism time-of-life when the body could process glucose (sugar) effectively.

You can play around at the gym and do an hour of steady-state, magazine-reading paced cardio (where you have to starve to get any results) and still experience the slowly creeping negatives of Metabolic Syndrome. Or the Sprint 8 Cardio Protocol can become the most effective weapon in your arsenal to fight Metabolic Syndrome during the aging.

Do you have 20 minutes, three-days-a-week? If you do, let's get started.

Case Study, Dr. Dave Woynarowski

Dr. Dave Woynarowski (below) is one of my heroes. As a physician and certified personal trainer, he has spent a lifetime helping others and sets the bar high for others to follow. Dr. Dave is a highly trained internal medicine specialist who practices what he preaches.

Dr. Dave is an athlete who has run marathons and shorter-distance races all over the world. He places in the top percentile of his age group. He has been a weight lifter for many years, and also practices Jiu-Jitsu and Catch wrestling.

He served as Associate Professor of Medicine at Hershey Medical Center. Dr. Dave has been the featured speaker for conference held American Academy of Anti-Aging Medicine, and he is one of the world's foremost authorities on supplemental nutrition physiology and telomeres. I highly recommend Dr. Dave's newsletter at *www.drdaveshealthsecrets.com*

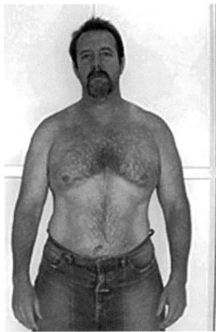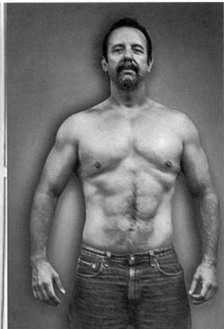

Much of the information in this chapter on telomeres comes from Dr. Dave's presentations and his book, *The Immortality Edge.*

Dr. Dave does Sprint 8 and teaches it to others. He has an excellent exercise plan in Chapter 3, *The Immortality Fitness Plan*, which includes the Sprint 8 Cardio Protocol.

Dr. Dave and the authors, Greta Blackburn, and Dr. Michael Fossel write:

In designing our fitness program, we looked for exercise that would absolutely provide the most fitness with the least damage. The fitness program we decided was best is derived from a tried and tested form of interval training called "Ready, Set, Go! Synergy Fitness," which was created by one of our expert advisers, Phil Campbell, a world-famous athlete and fitness trainer who started writing fitness manuals and managing health clubs more than thirty years ago. This exercise program involves a mixture of high-intensity bursts of exercise with moderate-intensity active recovery periods. Not only does our program produce the best results in the shortest time (twenty minutes), it also accomplished this with the least bodily stress -- and the least telomere shortening.

Next time you see one of those Nike ads featuring the stars of track and field, pay attention to how different the sprinters look from the marathoners. The sprinters have more developed muscles than the lean-bodied people who are running for hours at a time. It turns out that short bursts of high-intensity exercise builds muscle. The human body is designed to create new muscle fibers that can meet the demands of speed and explosive movement, (Woynarowski, D. (2001) *The Immortality Edge, Realize the Secrets of Your Telomeres,* Wiley p.84).

Dr. Elizabeth Blackburn Wins Nobel for Telomere Research

Dr. Elizabeth Blackburn is famous for her award-winning research with Carol Greider and Jack Szostak. They co-discovered telomerase, the enzyme that replenishes the telomeres at the ends of our chromosomes so our genetic data are protected. In Dr. Blackburn's book with Dr. Elissa Epel, *The Telomere Effect, Living Younger, Healthier and Longer,* (Grand Central Publishing 2017), the authors thoroughly discuss telomeres in understandable terms, and they describe the impact of exercise-induced inflammation and how this actually benefits the body at the cellular level.

Drs. Blackburn and Epel explain critical information in understanding how exercise actually heals the body even when the purpose of exercise is to stress the body and create microtrauma, or slightly injure the muscle at the cellular level. They explain:

> *Exercise leads to myriad beautiful intracellular changes. Exercise causes a brief stress response, which triggers an even bigger restorative response.* ***Exercise damages molecules, and damaged molecules can cause inflammation. However, early on in a bout of exercise, exercise induces autophagy, the Pac-Man-like process that eats up damaged molecules. This prevents inflammation.*** *Later in the same exercise session, when there are too many damaged molecules, and autophagy can no longer keep them under control, the cell dies a quick death (called apoptosis), in a cleaner way that doesn't lead to debris and inflammation.* ***Exercise also increases the number and quality of those energy-producing mitochondria. In this way, exercise can reduce the amount of oxidative stress. After exercise, when your body is recovering, it is still cleaning up cell debris, making cells healthier and more robust than before exercise.*** (Blackburn, E. Epel, Elissa (2017), *The Telomere Effect, Living Younger, Healthier and Longer.* Grand Central Publishing p179).

In essence, when we do the highest-intensity exercise like Sprint 8, we are intentionally starting an inflammation response in our muscles. The body reacts and adapts to this by getting stronger and pushing the inflammation-response threshold higher and higher. This is positive. It means your stronger body can endure much more stress than your sedentary body.

Those who do not exercise are in a bad position because simply living life becomes strenuous to the body and simple physical activities can induce excessive inflammation, which can become chronic inflammation over time.

Bad things happen fast to your health when your body is constantly inflamed. Simple activities of life shouldn't cause inflammation. However, when people choose not to exercise, their muscles become weak. Weak muscles can become inflamed with simple low-intensity activities.

Even for those who exercise regularly, moderate-intensity exercise doesn't create the microtrauma to the muscles anywhere close to sprint cardio. Moderate-intensity exercisers are better off than those who don't exercise, but they may be falling significantly below their potential in getting results for time spent.

If you do sprint cardio regularly and push the inflammation threshold high as possible, normal activities of life don't inflame your muscles. Even low-intensity exercise, and perhaps even moderate-intensity exercise becomes a non-inflammation producing activity to you. In essence, Sprint 8 is a tool to intentionally and systematically inflame the muscles that push the inflammation trigger to the highest level possible.

Sprint XC Skiing and sprint swimming are excellent ways to do Sprint 8

Sprint 8 at home on a treadmill and Matrix compact suspension elliptical

8

The Sprint 8 Cardio Protocol

Sprint 8 can be done in many different ways. It is a flexible training platform designed to reach the four exercise-induced growth hormone release benchmarks so you get the best results in the shortest amount of time.

Sprint 8 is totally flexible because it works on any variety of different exercise machines found in most clubs and fitness centers, or it can be performed with just your body -- sprint skiing, sprint swimming, or sprint running.

Whatever your preferred manner of cardio training, almost every method can be used for Sprint 8. Some of the best methods include the elliptical, recumbent cycle, treadmill, upright cycle, rowing machine, stair stepper (but covering two steps with each high-knee step), actual climbing stairs, and any host of other options that will get your heart rate up and get you winded in 30 seconds or less.

If the exercise method gets you totally winded in 30 seconds or less, it can be used for Sprint 8. The Krankcycle is a great way to accomplish Sprint 8 for those with leg impairment or disability.

Using an all-out, maximum effort swimming sprint for 25 meters and holding on to the side for the active recovery can be used for most swimmers. A very fit, technique-trained, advanced swimmer may have to sprint swim 25 meters, flip and sprint back 25 meters for one cardio rep to achieve the growth hormone release benchmarks.

You can use cross-country skiing sprints to do Sprint 8. And of course you can always simply sprint run -- as in running on a track, trail, road or in a park. You can apply the Sprint 8 design to other exercise styles, as well -- as long as the cardio sprint gets you totally winded in 30 seconds or less and you recruit a lot of *fast-muscle fiber* so your heart muscle has to work hard trying to oxygenate *all three muscle fiber types*.

Sprint 8 on Cardio Units

Select your favorite piece of cardio equipment for a two-minute warm up set on a very low-level (level 1 or 2). If your favorite piece is the treadmill, obviously you are a runner. The Sprint 8 Protocol on a treadmill is more complex because the technology adjustment to determine the velocity of movement takes place before the beginning. When you are using an elliptical, recumbent or upright cycle for example, you can make velocity adjustments as you go.

Even if you are a runner, I recommend *learning the feel* of Sprint 8 on a recumbent bike or an elliptical unit. Once you experience what a 30-second, maximum-effort, all-out cardio sprint is during Sprint 8, this will help you learn the technology settings necessary to achieve all four growth hormone release benchmarks.

When you are using an elliptical, recumbent or upright cycle, you can make self-adjustments with velocity during the cardio sprint to achieve maximum effort. On a treadmill, the button-push touch with your finger before the cardio sprint (for the resistance and speed) takes away the ability to use velocity for max effort. Sprint 8 on a treadmill works great, it just takes time to learn the technology settings.

After a two-minute warm up, you begin cardio sprint #1. Each cardio sprint has the goal of making it the full 30 seconds with all-out, hard and as fast-as-you-can-go intensity. That is, you work so hard on the sprints that you literally can't make it any further at that level of intensity longer than 30 seconds. Your target is 30 seconds of all-out action on whatever exercise tool (treadmill, upright bike, elliptical) you are using. Your heart rate will elevate dramatically and your muscles will start burning at the half way point, but push on and hit the full 30-second mark for the cardio sprint.

Warning: Sprint cardio, without question, is the most demanding form of cardio and you should ask your physician to clear you for anaerobic exercise. If someone's arteries are almost clogged with plaque, anaerobic exercise like Sprint 8, and even lower intensity aerobic exercise, can be very dangerous. If you have a heart condition, please clear this with your physician. I've never had a major problem with Sprint 8 in my 30 years of teaching it other than a few cases of weakness from exercise-induced hypoglycemia -- a condition characterized by abnormally low blood glucose (blood sugar). Diabetics typically understand this condition, but it can also happen to non-diabetics doing Sprint 8. A couple of crackers, a glass of orange juice, or a banana (my personal favorite) with 5-minutes of rest seems to resolve exercise-induced hypoglycemia in many cases, *(http://www.diabetes.org/living-with-diabetes/treatment-and-care/blood-glucose-control/ hypoglycemia-low-blood.html#sthash.iJbaoZvr.dpuf).*

One of the reasons I recommend starting Sprint 8 with two reps and slowly, progressively building up to all eight reps is most people have never exercised this hard before -- or it's been a while since playing sports in high school. Generally, two cardio sprint reps is plenty hard for the *first* Sprint 8 workout.

If you haven't been doing any type of sprinting in your training, the *fast-muscle fiber* in your muscles have become smaller, and they are weak relative to your *slow muscle fiber*. This fact alone somewhat regulates your ability to go too fast when starting Sprint 8 on a cardio unit. Sprint running on a track is different. You can easily go fast enough to rip a hamstring, calf or achilles. Learning Sprint 8 on a cardio unit will provide a certain amount of protection from this as you learn how to do Sprint 8 safely and build your *fast-muscle fiber* to a point it can support sprint running.

Please remember that your experience with interval training, HIT or HIIT is still much less intense than sprint-intensity cardio. Interval training steps up intensity and may recruit and strengthen some *IIa fast-muscle fiber,* but most likely, your *IIa fast-muscle fiber* (moves *five* times faster than the slow) and *IIx fast-muscle fiber* (moves *ten* times faster than the slow) are smaller and weaker than their potential. This simply means, be smart and ease into Sprint 8. It takes time to condition your *fast-muscle fiber* and the anaerobic process of your heart muscle. Be smart -- start with just two cardio sprint reps your first time.

Velocity of Movement

The main focus that provides the benefits of the Sprint 8 Protocol is during each cardio sprint, and creating the ability to move hard and fast at the highest level of intensity.

When using a machine for Sprint 8, the resistance level on the unit is important as you want to find a balance of intensity from two factors, *velocity of movement* and *resistance.* This balance provides the best sprinting zone.

Remember it's the Sprint 8, not the Fast 8 or the Power 8, it has to be hard and fast, but err on the side of fast.

Achieving high velocity with good resistance during each cardio sprint is vital to the success of the protocol. This effort requires a commitment on your part to peddle, pump, run or swim each cardio sprint hard-as-you-can and intense enough to get totally winded in 30 seconds or less. About every ten seconds during the 30-second cardio sprint tell yourself *step it up*, otherwise you may be subconsciously pacing and not know it.

Pacing is the Enemy of Intensity

Each cardio sprint calls for full intensity for 30 seconds. Coaching Sprint 8, I constantly say, *Pacing is the enemy of intensity. Don't let your body pace.*

As you begin to add additional cardio sprints as you build up to all eight reps in the fully mature Sprint 8 Protocol, you will accumulate fatigue along the way. But don't let that keep you from making the most of each cardio sprint. The goal is not to do all eight reps. The goal is, to do each sprint right with all-out, *fast-fiber recruiting* intensity, fighting the human desire to pace.

Pacing means you have dropped off some muscle fiber from the process so your heart muscle is working with less intensity.

The ability to hit each cardio sprint with all-out effort is as much mental and emotional, as it is physical. Initially it may be hard to rev back up for the next cardio sprint, but if you mentally approach each cardio sprint one-at-a-time, this seems to help. In other words, don't think about doing all eight reps.

The goal is to show up, get dressed, and get on the cardio unit for rep number one. After years of doing Sprint 8, I've never found it enjoyable -- until I'm finished. But man-o-man, is life great when it's done!

Although the Sprint 8 Protocol is flexible, there are a few absolutes. One of these is the 30-second mark for the cardio sprints. You have to max out at the 30-second point. It must be 30 seconds of effort so strong that you can't go longer than 30 seconds. Otherwise, you have paced. And pacing is the enemy of intensity.

The intensity has to be all-out for 30 seconds. If you stop the cardio sprint at 30 seconds but you could have gone to 33 seconds, this is a mistake because the intensity wasn't high enough. You paced.

To get the full impact and benefit of Sprint 8, you'll need to raise the intensity level; pedal, run or move as fast-as-you-can-go while the machine is set on a reasonably high resistance level so you get totally winded. You'll want to stop around 10 to 15 seconds – but fight, and keep fighting. Find a way to hang on for 30 seconds. This is a cardio sprint.

Maintaining maximum intensity for 30 seconds is tough. Over the course of a few workouts you will learn how to hit that 30 second mark with maximum effort from start to finish. If you do a cardio sprint correctly, you will feel like you are running out of gas before the 30-second mark as the pain level builds up, but hold on. Fight to reach the 30-second mark.

Jerry Bowyer of Jerry Bowyer Research has an excellent description of what it takes to achieve Sprint 8 intensity. He writes:

> *I find that in order to recruit all the muscle fibers, I have to recruit emotions. I imagine that one of my kids is under attack up at the top of the hill, and I have to get to them asap to save them.*

In many respects, Sprint 8, if done correctly, will be the hardest training program you've ever done. I wish I could say it becomes easier over time. It doesn't. I wish I could say that it gets better over time. I can't. While you may tolerate it better over time, Sprint 8 never gets easy. It's always hard, but it always works.

If you are looking for easy, this isn't the place. But if you're looking for getting the best results possible in a realistic time-efficient framework, you have found it.

Active Recovery

In between each cardio sprint is a period of *active recovery*. This is a resting recovery where you keep moving (active), but at a recovery pace. You don't stop moving - you simply lower your intensity level way down to the warm-up level.

Coming down from a hard, all-out, 30 second cardio sprint is not instant. It takes a few seconds to safely reach the active recovery pace.

The active recovery is 90 seconds in length. As soon as the 90 seconds are up, you start the next 30-second cardio sprint again. Once you are conditioned over time, and are ready for all eight reps, the 30-seconds on / 90-seconds off is repeated for eight reps.

Researchers report; *it appears that this kind of exercise protocol with* ***Active Recovery phases between the intervals may promote anabolic processes***, (Wahl, P. (2014) *Active vs. passive recovery during high-intensity training influences hormonal response.* Int J Sports Med. 2014 Jun;35(7):583-90.

You are trying to recover at the pace of a casual-paced walk. ***It's a mistake to make the 90 seconds low-intensity cardio.*** If you rush the 90-second recovery, you won't be recovered enough to go all-out during the next sprint.

Cool Down

When you finish the last cardio sprint and complete the last 90-second active recovery, at this point, add an additional 60 seconds to cool down. This will complete the 20-minute protocol.

Just as your body needs a warm-up period, it also needs a cool down period. For the Sprint 8 cool-down, reduce your effort dramatically, moving to a slow recovery pace before getting off your exercise machine. In effect, this slow down will let your heart rate come down from its high on a slope instead of dropping it off a cliff.

When getting off the machine, you may notice that your legs feel different. This is because most people aren't accustomed to recruiting and working all *three muscle fiber types* during training. Sprint 8 will never get easy. You get to a point where you tolerate anaerobic exercise better, but it's still never easy. If someone thinks Sprint 8 isn't extremely hard, it's simple, he/she didn't do it right.

Ground-Based Sprint 8

There are two conceptual methods to do the Sprint 8 Protocol, *body-weight supported* (on a cardio machine), and *ground-based* (running sprints carrying your full body weight). Ground-based Sprint 8 changes the 30-second cardio sprint time because sprint running is much more intense. The cardio sprint can be 10 to 20 seconds. What's important here is to know why there is a difference in the time factor between the running sprints and doing sprint-cardio on a machine.

Sprint 8 on a cardio unit requires the all-out, maximum-effort, full 30-second cardio sprint since part of your body weight is supported by the machine. This lessens the intensity. This isn't bad. Even if you are an experienced runner, starting Sprint 8 on a cardio machine can be a lot safer until you have strengthened your *IIa fast-muscle fiber* and your *IIx super-fast muscle fiber*.

When running the Sprint 8, you are essentially throwing your full body weight forward several feet with every foot strike. This places a huge force on the glutes, hamstrings, and calves when you haven't spent the time building up those muscles to prepare for sprint running. It's very easy, even predictable, that a strain will happen unless you have progressively strengthened the *fast-twitch muscles* propelling sprint running. This is why it's best to begin Sprint 8 on a cardio unit.

Don't Miss This Point When Running Sprints

There is a big difference between cardio sprinting and running sprints on the ground. When doing Sprint 8 on a cardio unit, you are riding the machine and this lessens the intensity — so it takes 30 seconds during the cardio sprint to accomplish the four growth hormone release benchmarks. It takes less time when running the Sprint 8 on the ground.

When using cardio equipment, the hamstrings are somewhat protected because the legs are not fully extended during the movement. They are not getting the absolute extension they would get in ground-based sprint running.

Did you know there is a significant difference between sprinting on a treadmill and sprinting on the ground? A treadmill lessens intensity when sprint running because you are riding a machine. Great for the knees and joints, but less intense.

When sprinting on a treadmill, your foot strikes the surface with the intensity to raise your body *upward* a couple of inches as the treadmill moves the surface under you. With ground-based sprint running, it's much more intense because you are throwing your body not just *upward* with each foot strike, you are throwing your body *forward* several feet. This means a 60-meter sprint in 8 seconds is as intense as an all-out treadmill sprint for 30 seconds.

Eight Reps Get's it Done

When you progressively, over time, build to all eight cardio sprints, this is the fully mature Sprint 8 Protocol. If you ever feel you need more than eight cardio sprints -- this means you didn't do it right.

This is a red flag that you are not getting anywhere close to the intensity of sprint cardio. Eight cardio sprints at maximum intensity should leave you -- as well as every human being alive -- totally drained.

In fact, early on, you should be going hard and fast, by the second or third cardio sprint you are questioning not only your sanity, but whether or not you can make the next rep.

Your velocity during the cardio sprint needs to be as *fast-as-you-can-go*, but it has to be very hard with resistance too. During the Sprint 8 Challenge class, if a Sprint 8 rookie says, *I think I can do one more than eight.* I won't have to say a word. The rest of the class will laugh and someone will say, *raise the intensity up one or two levels and see if that helps.*

This always makes the point -- if you ever think you need to do more than eight reps, you didn't do it right.

Eight reps is the fully mature Sprint 8. Trying to do more than eight reps, makes it less. Even thinking about doing more than eight reps means someone has held back and paced, and did not recruit *all three muscle fiber types* during the cardio sprints.

Remember from *Chapter 1,* your brain thinks it's doing you a favor to pace and do things with *slow-muscle fiber* (including exercise and even play sports) in the *endurance energy system.* Your brain thinks it is helping you to conserve the *fast-muscle fiber* in case you need it for an emergency later. When you do Sprint 8, it is so demanding, your brain knows that you'll need fluid, nutrition and sleep to totally recover your fast-muscle fiber, and pacing (consciously or subconsciously) is what the body does naturally -- unless you focus on *not* pacing.

Exercise Choice

There are quite a few different exercises you can use for Sprint 8. You can use Sprint 8 in your club, fitness center, your home gym, your swimming pool, the stairwell at your workplace, or at the hotel when you are on a business trip.

If you workout at a fitness club, you should have quite a few options, as far as which cardio equipment you may want to use for a Sprint 8 workout. Let's look at some of the readily available exercise tools you can use for Sprint 8

Recumbent Cycle

The recumbent cycle is the recommended way to learn the intensity of cardio sprinting. For runners, the recumbent cycling movement works extremely well to strengthen the exact muscles that propel the movement of running -- except you are giving your skeleton a day off.

A recumbent cycle will allow endurance athletes to out work the training plan or the competition with speed workouts, while safely protecting the hamstrings. And you will be giving your skeleton a day off from pounding the pavement that causes a lot of pre-event stress fractures, and over-use injuries.

The recumbent cycle in the slow-twitch world is nothing for healthy adults. Most people can do the recumbent for hours and not get much out of it.

In the fast-twitch world however, I don't care how conditioned you are, very few people can do all eight reps on a recumbent cycle the first time -- if they do Sprint 8 correctly.

You simply start pedaling for a warm-up of three minutes on a low level (like level 1 or 2) before the first cardio sprint. Then you raise the level anywhere between level 6 to 15. Now pump like crazy for a 30 second all-out cardio sprint.

Pump as fast-as-you-can-go, right up to the 30-second finish. If you feel like you just barely made the 30 seconds and, perhaps, even started to slow down the last few seconds no matter how hard you tried -- **COUNT THAT SPRINT**. You did it right!

If you could have gone longer than 30 seconds, sorry, don't count it. You paced that cardio sprint, and pacing is the enemy of intensity.

After the cardio sprint, slow down to a nice-and-easy recovery pace at the warm-up level (typically 1 to 2 level resistance) to recover for a full 90 seconds. This is a full cardio sprint segment.

You might think that a recumbent cycle is an easier option than the standard stationary cycle since you get to recline your body when you ride. However, when you are in a reclined position you have to elevate your big thigh muscles and this makes the recumbent ride as tough as (or tougher) than the regular upright cycle.

Upright Cycle

The upright cycle offers a great Sprint 8 workout. However, there are a couple of things you need to know.

An upright bike closely resembles the cycles you would see in the *tour de France* and at bike stores like BGI in Indianapolis, one of the largest bike stores in the US where I teach a Sprint 8 class for the public every January.

You need to know these bikes are made for efficiency -- efficient bikes to make outdoor cycling easier to cover distance faster -- this also significantly lessens intensity. The better the bike, the more efficient it makes pedaling. This means achieving sprint-intensity is very difficult, UNLESS (and this is a tough one) -- unless you take the efficiency out of the machine by sitting as upright-as-possible during the 30-second cardio sprint.

You can lean forward during the 90 second active recovery and tap into the efficiency of the machine to recover, but to make the cardio sprint intense enough to reach the four growth hormone release benchmarks, stay upright.

It looks funny I know. But after a couple of sprint cardio reps upright with constant intensity on your legs, you won't care what you look like. You'll just want it over. Now you're doing Sprint 8.

Bike

Just like doing Sprint 8 on an upright cycle, Sprint 8 on an outdoor bike is possible with a little creativity. The problem is, the more efficient the machine, the more difficult it is to achieve the sprint-intensity level required in Sprint 8.

Efficiency of the machine makes it easier. We need Sprint 8 to be hard. You have to get winded in 30 seconds or less during the cardio sprint or you have paced. Sprint cycling up a hill without gearing to the most efficient setting and sitting upright during the cardio sprint can help make it more intense. But the better the bike you have, the more difficult it is to achieve the four Sprint 8 benchmarks.

You can do Sprint 8 during a long ride. In fact, you can dramatically improve your cycling performance with Sprint 8 by strengthening the *fast-muscle fiber* that propels cycling movements.

Sprint 8 on a bike will build your endurance by multiplying energy-producing mitochondria at the cellular level. Dr. Martin Gibala's research shows that you can actually double endurance capacity in three workouts a week in two weeks time.

Mountain biking is golden! Sprint 8 is similar in many respects to hard, all-out, mountain biking -- if you go as hard as you can and get totally winded in 30 seconds or less. Just remember the active recovery rule for Sprint 8. If you aren't recovering in between the cardio sprints, you won't be able to put full sprint-intensity into the next sprint.

It takes a little creativity to work in a Sprint 8 workout during a long ride, or when mountain biking. But it can be done. And you will enjoy the benefits of significantly improved endurance and stronger fast-muscle fiber in your legs. It only takes cycling sprints two weeks (at three-times-a-week) to double endurance capacity. Throwing in a Sprint 8 during the ride is worth the effort.

I'll admit, your friends will laugh if they see you sitting upright on your bike sprinting as hard as you can (unless you tell them about Sprint 8 and challenge them to do Sprint 8 with you).

Elliptical

An elliptical cardio unit (found in most fitness clubs worldwide) is a great way to do Sprint 8, especially if the unit is made for Sprint 8 like the Matrix Fitness XI and Vision Fitness cardio units.

The elliptical unit allows you to get both lower body and upper body involved in the cardio sprint. This can mean even higher levels of sprint intensity because now your heart muscle and lungs have to work extremely hard to oxygenate all *three muscle-fiber types* in the lower and upper body at the same time.

In many respects, the elliptical is near the top of the list for being the toughest Sprint 8 workout of all. An elliptical Sprint 8 is second in intensity to actually running a ground-based Sprint 8 because of the full-body, muscle-fiber recruitment.

An elliptical unit allows you to achieve all-out intensity with the arms and legs pumping together. This is my personal favorite method for doing the Sprint 8 in a fitness club.

The elliptical Sprint 8 uses the same three-minute warm-up, 30 second cardio sprint, 90 second active recovery, times eight reps, and followed by a cool-down segment like the other cardio units.

In a cursory examination of the Sprint 8 research data, the subjects in the *General Group* who performed Sprint 8 on an elliptical unit manufactured by Johnson Health Tech, (parent company that owns Matrix Fitness and Vision Fitness, and has Sprint 8 as a featured program), experienced a slightly higher release of growth hormone than those using the recumbent and upright cycles.

This makes sense since the elliptical unit involves supporting your full-body weight, thus using your whole body during the cardio sprints. Using an elliptical unit will recruit all *three muscle fiber types* in your upper and lower body, as your heart muscle works very hard to oxygenate the muscles.

Although the elliptical unit is producing more growth hormone than the recumbent and upright cycles, it's interesting to note the results in body-fat loss, muscle gain, and weight loss were essentially the same. While it wasn't a focus of the study to compare the productivity of the different cardio machines, the research data is telling us when you significantly increase exercise-induced growth hormone (while reducing body fat without changing diets), you've reached the pinnacle of the exercise. You're getting all you can get out of that workout!

Releasing more growth hormone from an elliptical verses a recumbent cycle isn't necessarily going to yield better physical results. When you get to that level of physical improvement with Sprint 8, results will show regardless of which cardio equipment you choose.

Whether your favorite Sprint 8 is on an upright cycle, treadmill, or recumbent cycle, don't feel you need to use the elliptical unit because of the upper and lower body aspects. Great results are there with Sprint 8 on any machine -- if you can find 20 minutes, three-days-a-week.

Treadmill

The treadmill is one of the most common exercise machines found in almost every fitness center in the world. The treadmill provides a great way to run the Sprint 8.

As discussed in *Ground-Based Sprint 8* a few pages ago, the treadmill requires a full 30-second cardio sprint to do the job whereas sprint running on a track is based on distance rather than time. The distance is 60 meters or 70 yards when you can speed full speed.

Sprint 8 on the treadmill begins with a three-minute *warm-up*. The goal is to progressively RAMP UP to faster speeds during the warm up and get the body prepared for sprint speed.

Begin by walking 2 - 3 MPH. This is a comfortable walking pace for most people. Walk for approximately one minute. RAMP UP the speed and jog at 5-6 MPH for 15 - 30 seconds. RAMP DOWN and walk for 30 seconds. RAMP UP to 6 -8 MPH for 10 - 20 seconds. Then RAMP DOWN for a walk for approximately 30-seconds before the first cardio sprint.

For Cardio Sprint #1, RAMP UP the speed to 8-10 MPH for the first 30-second treadmill sprint. Once the 30-seconds sprint is accomplished, RAMP DOWN the speed to 2 - 3 MPH (walking pace) to finish out the 90-second active recovery (that officially began at the end of the 30-second sprint and the beginning of the RAMP DOWN process).

Once you have mastered the Sprint 8 segments (one fast 30-second cardio sprint with a 90-second active recovery), and you can run 8 sprinting reps at 10 -12 MPH, then you begin adding elevation to the treadmill deck to increase intensity.

The best treadmills to use are the ones made for the Sprint 8 -- the most demanding form of exercise on any cardio machine. Matrix Fitness and Vision Fitness have Sprint 8 as a featured cardio program and these units are made tough and durable to handle sprint cardio. Most cardio units are made for long / slow cardio. As a back up, a treadmill that allows you to quickly accelerate to 12 MPH may work. The ability of the treadmill deck to incline is also very important so you can continue adding intensity once you have reached the top treadmill speed.

Human beings can run faster than 20 MPH. Usain Bolt hit a top speed of 28 MPH for a short stretch during his 100-meter world record performance. Adding elevation makes the treadmill sprint more intense because you are now sprinting uphill.

It will take time to learn the technology controls of elevation and speed for Sprint 8 on a treadmill. Initially, it may be positive to do most of the cardio sprints on other cardio units and switch to the treadmill for the last two to four reps -- until you learn the programming adjustments.

Rowing

A rowing machine is somewhat like the elliptical in that it uses upper and lower body to propel the rowing movements.

The rowing action lets you work both the leg/hip region and the back at the same time. Some people make the mistake of putting most or all of the emphasis on the back. The legs/hips/glutes should be the *key* drivers in the rowing movement, and the back should be engaged more as a support muscle group.

Start off with moderate rowing action, at an easy pace, for a three minute warm up. When you hit the 30-second starting point, explode into some hardcore, intense rowing emphasizing the thighs to propel the full rowing movement.

Row as hard as you can for a full 30 seconds -- really rolling the action rapidly with violent thrusts from the legs on each stroke. Once you complete the 30-second cardio sprint, drop back to an easy, slow-rowing pace for the active recovery.

Stay with the slower pace recovery for 90 seconds. Remember to make the 90-second active recovery, all about recovery. If you try to make it cardio rather than recovery, you won't be able to put full intensity into the next rowing sprint.

If you are experienced with a rowing machine, start with two to four rowing sprint reps with maximin intensity (with good technique), and build up to all eight reps over time.

Stair Sprinting

Your sprinting doesn't have to be confined to the track or a machine in a gym. If you have access to a stairwell you can get in a superb Sprint 8 workout and be back in your office in time to eat a healthy lunch. How? By sprinting up the stairs.

When you climb the stairs in a Sprint 8 routine, focus on taking a deep step, eating up more than one step at a time and getting the thighs strongly involved. For your average stairwell, this means stepping up over 3 stairs in a single step. If you are tall or have short stairs, you might be able to do 4 steps, depending on how steep the stairs are.

Since you are going uphill, you don't have to radically sprint but climb at a pace that is close to sprinting as the elevation will make each succeeding step tougher. You want to move up the stairs as fast as you can. By sprinting uphill with your full body weight, you already have a heavy demand on the body, increasing velocity adds even more intensity.

Focus on the balance of the uphill movement and speed to make the most of the stair climbing sprint. Make each step you take a big one, but not so big that you lose your balance. Sprint up enough steps that it takes 30 seconds. This becomes your 30-second sprint #1. The active recovery will be the trip back down the stairs -- take the full 90 seconds coming down -- breathing deep and controlled to recover. For the fully mature Sprint 8, you would need seven more reps.

Start off stair climbing with two stair sprints. Gradually build to eight reps

Moving your body up the stairs at a rapid pace is quite challenging (as well as stimulating) and will rapidly elevate your metabolism. For your warm-up phase before going all out, climb the stairs for a couple of minutes at a normal pace, taking just a step or two instead of the big steps.

There are a couple of places where stair sprinting works especially well -- at the hotel when you are on a trip (provided the hotel has several flights of stairs). You don't need to wait for the gym to open to workout -- you can get in a full Sprint 8 right in the stairwell. The other place is at work if you have a multi-level office building (or one is nearby). You can get in a quick Sprint 8 workout on your lunch or break period. That's right, a full workout right in your own office (if you have the stairs).

Running the Sprint 8

Running the Sprint 8 on a track or out on a field is one of the most intense activities your body can engage in. Both sprint running and jumping are supreme, high-demand movements and push your body to the edge physically. Running the Sprint 8 is at the top of the list for the most intense method of doing the protocol.

There are two elements in the Sprint 8 Cardio Protocol needing consideration when sprint running; the time factor and the hamstring factor.

If you choose to run Sprint 8, you can finish the cardio sprints quicker because you only need 10 to 15 seconds for each cardio sprint. However, the hamstring factor means that warm up takes significantly longer than three minutes. A three-minute warm up is perfect for a cardio unit Sprint 8 because the risk of hamstring injury is far less.

Running sprints means you are taking your full body weight and propelling it forward 5 to 6 feet with every step, and this is a tremendous amount of force applied directly on each hamstring.

Sprint 8 on a track or field is covering a distance of 60 meters (or 70 yards) as fast as you can AFTER you have performed a comprehensive warm up that includes several ramp up sprints, and a dynamic mobility warm up (that isn't required with other methods).

The active recovery is the same when sprint running (90 seconds) as it is with the Sprint 8 on a cardio unit. If you walk back to the starting line for the next sprint, that typically takes 60 to 90 seconds. You continue to repeat the sequence of 60-meter sprints and a 90-second return to the starting line for eight reps.

Getting Started

The current condition of the fast-fiber in your legs and the anaerobic conditioning of your heart muscle determine how quickly you can work into a full Sprint 8 workout.

It is very important to realize sprint running is a totally different animal than jogging and totally different (and much more intense) than interval training. Maximum-effort, sprint running is the most intense Sprint 8 of them all.

Even if you are running a lot of mileage right now, please don't assume you can step right into a full-speed Sprint 8 on the track. The more mileage you do means you have strengthened your *slow-muscle fiber* and the aerobic process of your heart muscle. If you haven't been working your *fast-muscle fiber* along the way, both types of *fast-muscle fiber* are small and weak. And it takes time to progressively build them to where you can sprint fast without injury.

Please note; general strengthening of your legs muscle won't prepare you for sprint running. General strength means slow-moving, *slow-twitch muscle fiber* strength building and this is entirely different from the strength you need for sprint running.

Even running intervals won't prepare you for sprint running because you aren't working the *super-fast IIx muscle fiber.* You have to slowly build the *IIx fiber* with incrementally faster running. This will take 6 to 8 weeks to progressively build to an interval training pace before going full speed.

As with the Sprint 8 on cardio machines, the best way to start actual run sprinting is incrementally. You start with eight 60-meter jogging-pace runs. If you are a runner, you can start at a faster pace for eight reps. The following Progressive Sprint 8 Running RAMP UP CHART is a good guide for an experienced runner who has successfully used interval training speeds for a period of time, and who is aerobically and anaerobically conditioned.

Sprint 8 Running

Warm up

Light Jog *(3 to 5 minutes)*
Dynamic Mobility Drills (20 to 30 minutes)
  Drills are light-plyometrics, 15 yards & walk back to start
* Side-to-side slides (switch direction every three slides)
* A skips (Skipping forward with knee coming to waist level)
* B skips (A skips but add kick on the up knee moving down)
* High knees
* Butt Kickers
* Karaoke
* Tapioca (Similar to Karaoke except feet stay low to ground. Move feet quickly and quietly)

Sprinting Ramp Up Chart

1st Sprint

Begin at brisk jogging pace and build up to
50% speed during the 70 yards (60 meters)
Slow down for 10+ yards
Walk back during 90-second recovery

2nd Sprint

Begin at 40% speed; build to 60% speed

3rd Sprint

Begin at 50% speed; build to 70% speed

4th Sprint

Begin at 60% speed; build to 80% speed

5th Sprint

Begin at 70% speed; build to 90% speed

6th Sprint

Build up to 95% - 100% speed. Get fluid.

7th Sprint
95% - 100% speed. Listen to your hamstrings every rep

8th Sprint
95% -100% speed. Take time slowing down.

Cool-down
Walk for a 3 minute cool down

The sprints should be performed at a progressive, build-up, interval training pace -- gradually getting faster and faster over time. Ease into all-out sprint running by moving up the intensity dial slightly every workout until you are sprinting full speed.

Whether you are 17 or 70, exercise intensity is relative to age and conditioning. Your anaerobic conditioning program should be fun, fast and effective -- at any age. However, keep in mind that running the Sprint 8 is very demanding and can be hazardous to your health. It's important to continue building the *fast-muscle fiber* propelling the sprinting movements -- progressively and incrementally, over several months -- to reduce the risk of injury.

If you haven't been exercising for quite some time, you will want to begin your workouts with four to eight reps of 50 percent speed/intensity. My experience is it takes six to eight weeks of progressively strengthening the *fast-muscle fiber* in your legs to be able to achieve the 95 - 100 percent speed/intensity level without injury to hamstrings, glutes, achilles, or calve muscles. This applies to athletes and adults of all ages -- unless you are currently running sprints.

The Adaptation Principle discussed in the introduction (your body adapts to the way you train) really applies here. You may have been running for 30 years You may have even been doing interval training and perhaps recruited, worked and strengthened some of your *fast-twitch IIa fiber*. However, if you haven't been recruiting your *super-fast IIx fiber* to help propel full-speed sprint running, your *IIx super-fast muscle fiber* isn't strong, and there is a significant risk of hamstring injury.

Once you have progressively strengthened your *fast-muscle fiber*, and when your body is ready, sprint full speed the last two reps. The following week, sprint the last three reps, then the last four reps (you get the idea).

After the 70-yard sprint and the 10 to 20 yard slow down, walk back to the starting line at a casual pace. Don't jog back to the starting line after the sprint. You need to get your *fast-muscle fiber* recovered so you can put more intensity into the next sprint. And don't rush the 90-second recovery. Take the full 90 seconds between each sprint to recover.

Note, this workout is for those who have been doing sprint running, and who have progressively built up *fast-muscle fiber* to tolerate this level of intensity. You don't want to walk out on a track and try performing Sprint 8 until you have gradually, patiently, and incrementally built up to this routine over a period of a several weeks. Rushing the progressive build-up period, increases risk of injury.

The speed-intensity output in these sprints is subjective. You have to figure how hard you are going and learn to estimate speed/intensity. The more you learn about your body during sprint running, the better the results will be. This requires you to gauge your all-out, 100-percent, speed/intensity effort, and make needed adjustments along the way.

Anaerobic Benefits the Aerobic

The Sprint 8 Protocol is a helpful tool for the long-distance runner. Dr. Stephen Boutcher reports healthy young and older adult men and women can **improve their cardiorespiratory fitness as much as 46 percent** in less than 15 weeks with this type of training, (Boutcher, S (2011), *High-Intensity Intermittent Exercise and Fat Loss J Obes.*868305. PMC2991639).

Not only will Sprint 8 significantly improve fitness, the anaerobic conditioning may address a very serious problem endurance runners face. Every year a small number of distance runners will push too hard and actually suffer heart failure during marathons. Needless to say this can be fatal.

Have you ever heard of a TRAINED, 100-meter sprinter dying from running a 100-meter sprint? I haven't, and I can't find one case where this has happened.

Distance runners training only the endurance energy system for long time periods are typically only using *slow-twitch fiber,* which means they aren't conditioning the anaerobic process of their heart muscle. There are two processes of the heart muscle. We should be conditioning both the aerobic process and the anaerobic process.

Long-distance runners seem to think their heart muscle is fully conditioned in their aerobic training. The aerobic process may be. But then they get into a marathon, in heat, and the heart muscle moves from the aerobic process (where they are conditioned) to the anaerobic process (where they are not conditioned), this can become dangerous. If a distance runner tries to push the heart muscle in the anaerobic system without having anaerobic conditioning, the results can be catastrophic.

Sadly, this happens almost every year -- runners die during marathons even though they've been training for months and years. This is tragic and quite possibly, preventable. Researchers report;

> *Of 3,718,336 total marathon participants over the 10-year study period, we identified 28 people (6 women and 22 men) who died during the marathon race and up to 24 hours after finishing, (Mathews SC (2012, Jul) Mortality among marathon runners in the United States, 2000-2009. Am J Sports Med. 40(7):1495-500).*

Three runners, in the same marathon died in 2009 during the Detroit Marathon/Half-marathon. Their ages, 26, 36 and 65.

Programming in *anaerobic conditioning* as part of the endurance training plan, may be a wise health and fitness improvement strategy. Only focusing on long-slow training, in my opinion, is dangerous because supreme aerobic conditioning can mislead a runner to think the heart muscle is strong and conditioned for anything. Obviously, it's not. The heart muscle is strong for long-slow aerobic work, but not for anaerobic work. A runner needs to add anaerobic conditioning during training to condition the heart muscle. The great news is that anaerobic conditioning doesn't take a lot of time. It only takes 20 minutes three-days-a-week.

Senior Games Sprinter, Charlie Baker, age 89 (above) holds many state records. He is nationally ranked # 4 in the US and #7 in the World with a long jump of 9'8." He is also ranked in the sprints, jumps and throws.

Bill Daprano, age 89, was inducted into the USATF Masters Hall of Fame for a lifetime of setting track & field records. Bill is ranked #2 in the US and #3 in the World in pole vault, and he is ranked in the jumps, sprints and throws.

Jeanne Daprano, age 79 is ranked #1 in the World in the mile. Jeanne was the first woman age 70 to break a 7-minute mile. Competing in the Women 75-79 masters group, she ran an indoor mile in 8:23. She is also ranked in #1 in the US in the 800 meters. With husband Bill, they have set 17 World Records in track & field.

Why is it masters athletes who train as sprinters, look, act, and feel 30-years younger. Let me tell you why. The sprint training they do releases exercise-induced growth hormone. Just attend the Finals in USA Masters Track & Field or Senior Games for the sprinting events. You will observe that Masters and Senior Games sprinters all look much young than their biological ages.

Canadian masters sprinter and hurdler, and author of the highly recommended book, *The Complete Book of Running -- How To Be a Champion from 9 to 90,* Earl Fee, age 89 (above), has set over 50 age group World Records. Competing in the Men's 400 meters, age 65-69 (below), he ran the sixth fastest time ever, 57.97 seconds. This distance is one lap around the track. Running 400 meters in less than one minute is impressive. This feat would be near impossible for most adults 30 years younger. The great majority of high school students couldn't beat his performance.

9

Enhancing Sprint 8

There are some things you can do to enhance the effectiveness of the Sprint 8 Cardio Protocol by maximizing the release of exercise-induced growth hormone. Research shows there are some nutrition-based tools available to help maximize your sprint cardio efforts. These tools are positive, but not absolutely necessary to the success of Sprint 8. Fitness writer James Fell hits the nail on the head:

> *Exercise first, diet later. We need to get past a reward mentality of thinking you deserve to eat unhealthy food after exercising. When you exercise you will find that you make wiser food choices.* (James Fell, www.bodyforwife. com. April 1. Breakfast Television. Retrieved 2 June 2016).

Sprint 8 Nutritional Enhancement

What you eat plays an important role in how your body responds to training as well as affecting your general health. The old saying about computers -- *garbage in, garbage out* is also true for what you eat. The opposite is also true -- eating quality food will build up your body, help to keep you healthy, trim and muscular. Eating smart will enhance your training. Here are a few unique elements for maximizing the results from the Sprint 8 Protocol.

PRE Sprint 8

L-glutamine, 2-grams

One banana

Dark Chocolate, one square 85% Cocoa *or greater*

Researchers show taking *2 grams of L-glutamine* will provide a benefit by facilitating the release of growth hormone. L-glutamine is an amino acid the body produces naturally. With people who exercise intensely, their levels of glutamine drop. Having an extra load on board prior to Sprint 8 can give the body a boost in performing the workout.

Web MD reports of this supplement in *Glutamine: Uses, Side Effects, Interactions, and Dosing:*

> Glutamine is the most abundant free amino acid in the body. Amino acids are the building blocks of protein. Glutamine is produced in the muscles and is distributed by the blood to the organs that need it. Glutamine might help gut function, the immune system, and other essential processes in the body, especially in times of stress. **It is also important for providing "fuel" (nitrogen and carbon) to many different cells in the body. If the body uses more glutamine than the muscles can make (i.e., during times of stress), muscle wasting can occur**, *(WebMD, http://www.webmd.com/vitamins-supplements/ingredientmono-878-glutamine.aspx?activeingredientid=878&).*

Web MD also reports that doses up to 40 grams of L-glutamine per day may be safe. In one study, researchers report after a marathon, glutamine levels drop significantly, and this is the reason so many people competing in marathons get a common cold after the event, (Castell (1997)*Some aspects of the acute phase response after a marathon race, and the effects of glutamine supplementation).*

Pre-workout glutamine supplementation has also been shown by researchers to reduce the post-exercise decline in blood glutamine levels, (Krzywkowski, (2001), *Effects of glutamine on exercise-induced changes in lymphocyte function).*

Clearly, those doing maximum-intensity sprint cardio need to pre-load and replenish post-workout nutrients used to generate energy during training. It's a reasonable fitness improvement strategy to enhance your training by supplementing with 2-grams of glutamine prior to Sprint 8. Nutritional fuel before training is wise. I also recommend my personal favorite, a banana to preload and reduce exercise-induced hypoglycemia.

Researcher George Schreiner Jr., MD, PhD, adds another pre-training tip shown to support mitochondria -- Baker's Bittersweet 85% (or greater) Dark Chocolate as it contains roughly 30 grams of *Epicatechin*. Please note, this is not milk chocolate. It has to be true dark chocolate.

I suggest to Sprint 8 Challenge class members to experiment with two grams of L-Glutamine, one banana, and one square of 85 percent or greater dark chocolate full of epicatechin. Researchers report:

> *Epicatechin enhances exercise capacity in mice ... aging has deleterious effects on modulators of muscle growth, and the consumption of modest amounts of the flavanol epicatechin can partially reverse these changes,* (Gutierrez-Salmean G. (2014 Jan) Effects of epicatechin on molecular modulators of skeletal muscle growth and differentiation. J Nutr Biochem. ;25(1):91-4.).

During the Sprint 8 - Liquid

During the Sprint 8, you want to stay hydrated. A study published in the *Journal of Strength and Conditioning Research* is quite specific about the role that water plays - **water affects athletic performance more than any other nutrient**, (Jones, L. (2008, March) *Active Dehydration Impairs Upper and Lower Body Anaerobic Muscular Power. J Strength & Conditioning Research. March 22 Active Dehydration).

Researchers in this study are taking data from athletes training with high intensity for *anaerobic strength and power,* and they report; *water* is a key factor for success in muscle building:

> **Sports performance requiring anaerobic strength and power can be impaired by inadequate hydration**. *Impairments as a result of dehydration may not only lead to reduction in performance but also increased susceptibility to musculoskeletal injury, strength and conditioning professionals must be aware that becoming voluntarily dehydrated can decrease anaerobic power,* (Jones (2008), Active *Dehydration*),

Bottom line -- if you are dehydrated you won't achieve the maximum benefits from any workout, especially Sprint 8 intensity workouts. And there is a chance you could even become injured as well.

Additionally, after a workout your muscles are weak and need a full rehydration. Failure to do that can impair the effectiveness of the workout on your body as it attempts to recover.

You especially want to be hydrated before your Sprint 8 workout even though it is a short time frame. This means hydrating with water prior to the workout, as well as during the workout. It's a good idea to have water handy, and use it. Researchers report:

> *We conclude that the exercise-induced growth hormone response decreases when exercise is performed without fluid intake,* (Peyreigne C. (2001) *Effect of hydration on exercise-induced growth hormone response*).

POST Sprint 8 -- Skip the High-Glycemic Carbs

One other very key factor - focus on limiting high-gylcemic sugar intake after Sprint 8 during the two-hour *Sprint 8 Synergy Window* discussed in Chapter 4, *The Ultimate Driver of Sprint Intensity*, pages 64- 65.

High-glycemic, fast-burning, candy-bar types of sugar interferes with the release of growth hormone. You don't want to short-circuit the effort you put in Sprint 8 or its benefits of releasing growth hormone. Eating a sugar-loaded candy bar or other high-sugar, high-glycemic carbs, will shut down circulating growth hormone and prevent you from receiving all the wonderful benefits during the *Two-Hour Synergy Window* after Sprint 8.

Sugar is probably not a healthy food anytime of day, but it's especially negative post-Sprint 8. The average American eats 156 pounds of sugar a year. This is a half pound of sugar a day. No wonder America is fat.

The CDC reports **69 percent of adults age 20 years and over are overweight or obese,** (*Obesity and Overweight.*(2016), Centers for Disease Control & Prevention, *http://www.cdc.gov/nchs/fastats/obesity-overweight.htm*).

According to the *American Heart Association*, the maximum amount of added sugar we should eat in a day are:

Men: 9 teaspoons

Women: 6 teaspoons

On average, Americans eat 48 teaspoons of sugar a day when the recommended number is less than 10.

Sugar is an inflammatory and lots of sugar does bad things to the body. This is especially true when attempting to maximize circulating exercise-induced growth hormone because of its negative interaction with refined sugar.

During the post-Sprint 8 time frame, you want to maximize, not minimize the growth hormone you released. After Sprint 8, get protein, not refined sugar.

Some intake of carbs is fine with the protein during this time, but make sure it is *not* high-glycemic, fast burn, candy bar types of sugar. These types of carbs on an empty stomach with surely spike insulin, and in turn, shut down growth hormone you want circulating as long as possible going after body fat.

In a recent conversation with Jim LaValle, a nationally recognized clinical pharmacist, author, board certified clinical nutritionist and founder of Metabolic Code Enterprises, his post training research-based recommendation is *Magnesium 300 mg, Vitamin C 500 mg, and CQ10 100mg.* Jim has authored 20 books concerning clinical nutrition, and he is one of the most knowledgeable experts in his field (http://www.jimlavalle.com/).

Sprint Intensity Increases Daily Protein Amount

It's well-known, protein utilization, and the need to replenish dietary protein increases during the recovery period after exercise. A high-protein meal *with minimal sugar*, or even a protein supplement containing 20 to 25 grams of protein *with minimal sugar* after Sprint 8 is a wise recovery strategy.

People who do endurance types of exercise need more protein than those who do not exercise. People who do sprint cardio need more protein than those who do endurance training in order to make the positive hormones it produces.

It's helpful to look at the research with endurance-training athletes versus strength, power and speed-training athletes to see what's happening with nutrition support for different levels of intensity. Doing Sprint 8 three times a week means you are training like an athlete. Researchers report:

> *The current recommended intakes of protein for strength and endurance athletes are 1.6 to 1.7 grams per kilogram and 1.2 to 1.4 g/kg per day, respectively,* (Fielding RA. (2002, Jul-Aug). *What are the dietary protein requirements of physically active individuals,* 2002, Jul-Aug, Nutr Clin Care).

Endurance training: 1-gram of protein X *50 percent of your body weight per day* (1.2 to 1.4 grams per *kilogram* a day).

Sprint training: 1-gram of protein X *75 percent of your body weight per day (*1.2 to 1.7 grams per kilogram a day).

For this reason, I placed an easy-to-remember estimate of the daily amount of protein when doing sprint cardio -- *75 percent of your body weight per day.*

The second aspect concerning the increased need for protein is your body can only process ***20 to 30 grams of protein per setting***. More than this won't kill you, it's just very expensive waste products.

In a formal position paper outlining the current energy, nutrient, and fluid recommendations for *active adults* and *competitive athletes* was published by the *Dietitians of Canada,* the *Academy of Nutrition and Dietetics,* and the *American College of Sports Medicine.* The joint recommendations report contained an *Evidence Analysis* section for common questions and answers about nutrition:

> **Question:** *In adult athletes, what is the effect of consuming protein on carbohydrate and protein-specific metabolic responses during recovery?*
>
> **Answer:** *Ingesting protein (approximately **20 grams to 30 grams** total protein, or approximately 10g of essential amino acids) during exercise or the recovery period (post-exercise) **led to increased whole body and muscle protein synthesis** as well as improved nitrogen balance,* (2016, Feb). p 6. *www.dietitians.ca/sports*).

Insulin Balance

Calories in versus calories out is not the whole story, explains Laura LaValle, Director of Dietetics, Progressive Medical Center.

Insulin is the big variable that makes calories impact every person differently. Insulin and growth hormone are interrelated. Releasing growth hormone with Sprint 8 does wonderful things for your body. However, the balance of insulin in your body can make or break the impact of circulating growth hormone once it is released.

Insulin has several critical functions in addition to its well-known role of managing excessive sugar consumed in the diet. Insulin is important in controlling how the body uses fats (lipid metabolism), and it facilitates the entry of protein (amino acids) into muscle. Insulin may be the most important hormone in controlling energy during exercise.

Just search the Internet and you will see numerous articles and news reports about bodybuilders injecting growth hormone and insulin to speed up muscle growth and reduce body fat. Not only is this extreme. It's deadly.

There's a better way to get the benefits of injecting hormones. Your body does all of these things naturally with anaerobic sprint cardio, followed by 20 to 25 grams of protein with very low sugar during the two-hours after training.

We need natural insulin. Without an adequate supply of insulin, the body's ability to filter dietary sugar from the blood is limited. When this condition first begins, researchers call it *insulin resistance.* As this condition progresses, it becomes *metabolic syndrome*, later it becomes *pre-diabetes,* then it becomes *diabetes* -- if dietary sugar and muscle-to-body-fat composition isn't managed.

Insulin resistance makes the body a fat-making factory. Individuals with high levels of body fat (usually 30 percent over ideal body weight) often develop a resistance to insulin. The heavier and more sedentary a person is, the greater the degree of *insulin resistance*, (Reaven., G. (2001, Jul). *Syndrome X,* 2001, Ochsner J. 3(3): 124–125. PMCID: PMC3385776).

The body reacts to this condition by increasing circulating insulin to levels higher than normal. This causes a cycle to occur that increases body fat even more. When individuals with insulin resistance eat sugary carbohydrates, normal processes are altered. Carbohydrates do not enter muscles normally.

They go to the liver and are turned into fat (rather than being used for energy as they should be). The end result: more body fat and less energy.

It is the high percentage of body fat relative to lean muscle weight that increases the cells' resistance to insulin, reports Nan Allison, licensed nutritionist and author of *Full & Fulfilled, The Science of Eating to Your Soul's Satisfaction*.

You can workout for hours, supplement with L-glutamine, and get eight hours of sleep, but if you blow it by eating excessive refined sugar or too many carbs causing your insulin levels to skyrocket (in order to metabolize heavy sugar in your blood), you just kissed the benefits of exercise-induced growth hormone release good-bye.

Resistance to insulin occurs mostly in overweight individuals. This is a serious medical condition and is usually the first step toward diabetes, hypertension, high cholesterol, and cardiovascular disease (Metabolic Syndrome).

Insulin resistance occurs long before these diseases appear. It occurs mostly in adults with abdominal obesity, general obesity, and family history. It also occurs in older adults who have lost muscular strength, (Rao, (2001). *Insulin resistance syndrome*).

This is why adults over age 90 have seen great results in clinical trials with strength training. Researchers measured the impact of being overweight (not obese, but merely overweight) on developing serious diseases. The researchers concluded, **the risk for chronic diseases (heart disease, colon cancer, diabetes) is approximately twenty times higher for overweight people. The risks for serious diseases increase relative to the degree individuals are overweight,** (Field. (2001), *Impact of overweight on the risk of developing common chronic diseases during a 10-year period, Brigham and Women's Hospital Boston*).

Calories in versus calories out is not the whole story, explains Laura LaValle, Director of Dietetics, Progressive Medical Center.

No Pain Killers Before or After Training

Ibuprofen (Advil and Motrin) and naproxen (Aleve and Naprosyn) are members of the NSAID family of drugs. NSAIDs act in the body to block chemicals involved in the inflammatory response. This reduces pain, but it also reduces the benefits of your workout. And not just a little. Think in terms of wasting the benefits of the workout. (Soltow, QA (2006) *Ibuprofen inhibits skeletal muscle hypertrophy in rats*. Med Sci Sports Exerc. 2006 May;38(5):840-6).

When we tinker with the natural process of the body recovering and healing after strenuous exercise, the inflammatory response is thrown off. For practical purposes, we took benefits from that workout and threw them out the window.

Studies have shown NSAIDs slow the rebuilding of muscle cells after exercise as well as disrupt healing of muscles, ligaments, tendons and cartilage, (Almekiders 1999, 2003). Another related study shows a vast reduction in bone and muscle strength when animals are treated with ibuprofen, (Kulick 1986).

Mental Stress Impacts Growth Hormone Release

Mental stress causes many physical reactions in the body, including an increase in somatostatin that is shown to shut down the benefits of exercise-induced growth hormone. In one study, researchers administered drugs to stop somatostatin release in mice just prior to the onset of stress. The drugs restored the growth hormone that had been halted by stress.

Although the subjects of this study were mice, it can be safely concluded that high stress levels will stop growth hormone release via somatostatin, (Pritzlaff. *Impact of acute exercise intensity on pulsatile growth hormone release in men,* 1999, J Appl Physiol (1985). 1999 Aug;87(2):498-504).

Rest & Recovery

Another element in making the most of your Sprint 8 training is getting adequate rest and recuperation to rebuild. A Sprint 8 workout can be quite demanding on the body as it pushes your body to the limit of its capabilities. It is equally important to allow time to build the body.

This is the key to long-term body conditioning success. It's a very basic formula, but perhaps the most overlooked aspect of training. Unfortunately in our busy culture, rest seems to be the last thing most people focus on. Marathon runner Ryan Shay's teammates indicated he would run on a treadmill until he collapsed, (Yabroff, J. (2007, Nov 19). *Giving It Everything They've Got. Newsweek*).

Sadly, Ryan Shay passed away in the middle of the New York City Marathon. The body can only handle so much challenge until it breaks down. Muscle does not grow during the training phase -- it's torn down during training. Tearing down the body frequently without significant recovery leads to injury and illness, weakening the immune system.

Important point; Doing Sprint 8 and even lifting weights does NOT make muscles stronger. The reason we work muscle during strength training is to create micro-fiber tears in the muscle. We are actually creating slight micro injuries in the muscles. When we sleep, the body adapts to the micro-fiber tears by healing back bigger and stronger.

We aren't stronger when we leave the fitness center. We are weaker. Strength training does NOT make us stronger. It creates the potential to become stronger, but that does not happen until we sleep.

Dr. Han Selye Adaptation Principle

Every principle in exercise, especially the ones concerning recovery are all based on Dr. Han Selye's theory of the *General Adaptation Syndrome -- in order to improve, you must balance challenge with recovery*.

Dr. Selye's Adaptation principles are taught in almost every medical and health discipline. Dr. Selye (1907- 1982) was a Hungarian endocrinologist who researched the hypothalamic-pituitary-adrenal axis, which are the same glands involved in releasing growth hormone.

He taught that the body adapts by changing specifically to the stress. Stress the muscles with exercise, for example, and the body adapts by building muscles bigger and stronger. Stress bones with exercise, and your skeleton adapts by taking calcium and other nutrients, sending them to the stressed bones to make them thicker and stronger.

With Sprint 8, you are stressing (or working), *all three muscle-fiber types* in your leg muscles, and your core. Sprint 8 on an elliptical unit, swimming or running sprints, you will be also be stressing (working) your upper body so when you sleep, *all three muscle-fiber types,* as well as most of your skeleton (that was engaged in the sprint cardio), will adapt by becoming stronger -- when you sleep.

You don't need to train with Sprint 8 every day. Three days-a-week gets the job done. Allowing a day's rest between Sprint 8 workouts is the best strategy. When you perform three demanding Sprint 8 workouts every week, you are getting some very challenging workouts and still giving your body four days to rest and recover. Planning for a day off in between Sprint 8 workouts is a wise fitness improvement strategy.

Power of Sleep

Just like planning for a day off between Sprint 8 workouts is wise, planning on getting adequate sleep is too. Sleep is fundamental. Sleep is crucial in getting maximum benefits from Sprint 8.

Sleep, particularly deep sleep in phase three and four, is the time when the healing (of the micro-fiber tears) and growth takes place. If you miss deep sleep one night and push through and do the Sprint 8 the next day, you will be stressing an already stressed and weakened body. This is one reason athletes experience a higher rate of upper respiratory infections, (Nieman DC. (2000), *Is infection risk linked to exercise workload? Med Sci Sports Exerc.* 32(7 Suppl):S406-11).

Dr. William Dement, author of the book *The Promise of Sleep*, points out we live in a *sleep-sick society,* where people short-change themselves and fall into *sleep debt*. Dement points out each person has a required amount of sleep and not getting that amount, puts the person into the state of *sleep debt*.

Since the body repairs and heals during sleep, the lack of adequate sleep keeps the body from recovering from sprint-intensity cardio. The author of *Take a Nap! Change Your Life,* sleep researcher Dr. Sara C. Mednick reports in a *Newsweek interview*:

> *Research on sleep deprivation shows that even at six hours a night, there are all sorts of changes in the body. Insulin rises to pre-diabetes levels. There's an increase in heart disease. Without sleep you don't learn. People deteriorate during the day. It's difficult to sustain productivity,* (Napping Your Way to the Top. Business Week. Nov 27, 2006)

None of the things *lack of sleep* causes are good. They are all detrimental. You need quality sleep to get the full benefits of Sprint 8.

The amount of sleep needed can vary. Generally, 7 to 12 hours of sleep are sufficient. If you are receiving less than 5 or 6 hours of sleep per night, you may be wasting part or all of your sprint-intensity effort, (www.nutrition-factor.com/workoutnono.htm).

When you are training hard with Sprint 8 to release growth hormone, you don't want to quench growth hormone production by not getting enough sleep. Lack of sleep makes your body become a fat-making machine as it causes the body to process sugar less effectively.

Bruce J. Ketchum, editor at *EndurePlus.com* notes:

> *A study, led by Eve Van Cauter, Ph.D., researcher at the University of Chicago Medical School in Chicago, IL, examined the effects of varied amounts of sleep on 11 men, ages 18 to 27. The men spent eight hours in bed per night (fully rested period) for the first three nights, four hours per night (sleep deprivation period) for the next six nights and 12 hours per night for the last seven nights (recovery period). Results showed that after being deprived of sleep, the men's **bodies metabolized glucose less efficiently**. Levels of the stress hormone cortisol were also higher during sleep deprivation periods than when the study subjects were fully rested. Elevated cortisol levels have been linked to development of memory impairments and age-related insulin resistance and may impair athletic recovery,* (Ketchurn, B.http://sportsmedicine.about.com/library/weekly/aa062800.htm iv www.dolfzine.com/p.358.htm).

Realize that each time you come up short in sleep, you put the brakes on your improvement. The benefits of Sprint 8 training becomes impaired if you don't get adequate sleep.

Athletes and people who exercise intensely experience sleeping longer and better (with more slow-wave sleep) than those who do not exercise. Due to the intensity of Sprint 8, you should experience more sleep and better sleep on Sprint 8 training days. I frequently hear this from people doing Sprint 8.

Peter Walters, Ph.D., CSCS, Professor of Applied Health Science, Kinesiology, Wheaton College recommends *Three Guidelines For Optimal Sleep* in a research paper *Sleep: the Athlete and Performance* (*http://www.wheaton.edu/Academics/ Departments/AHS/Faculty/Peter-Walters)*.

While Dr. Walters directs his paper towards athletes, you now fit this category for his three guidelines application -- since you are training all *three muscle-fiber types* and both processes of the heart muscle (aerobic and anaerobic) just like athletes train. Dr. Walters' three keys to good sleep, in pertinent part:

1. Identify And Obtain The Amount Of Sleep YOU Need.

The frequent recommendation, "you need to sleep at least eight hours per night," is simplistic and in many cases inappropriate. It reflects a statistical average, not a creed for all to follow.

*The amount of sleep someone needs is genetically determined and **varies considerably from person to person**. For example, Olympic gold medallist Dan Jansen slept an average of 10 hours per night prior to the 1994 Olympics in Lillehammer, Norway, while Bonnie Blair, holder of five gold medals, slept little more than six hours.*

2. Keep A Regular Sleep Schedule

*Practically all living people, animals, and even plants have a circadian or daily rhythm. This internal clock determines, among other things, when one feels sleepy and alert. **The circadian rhythm needs consistency** to perform efficiently. The importance of a consistent sleep pattern can be observed in individuals who do not have regular sleep schedules.*

Some experts believe the primary reason people who sleep longer on the weekends report feelings of increased lethargy on Mondays is that their internal clocks have been disrupted.

Inconsistent sleep patterns not only disrupt one's internal biological clock but also tend to increase the amount of time it takes to fall asleep.

3. Create An Optimal Sleeping Environment.

Four factors typify a high quality-sleeping environment: quiet, dark, cool, and comfortable. While humans can adapt to frequent and high levels of noise during sleep, such as traffic, airplanes, and trains, low levels of noise are associated with improved sleep.

*Researchers suggest that **65 degrees Fahrenheit is the optimal room temperature for sleep.** Although personal preference may deviate from this norm, temperature is an important sleep variable. A room either too hot or too cold can increase the amount of time it takes to fall asleep, The number of sleep disruptions throughout the night, and decrease the overall quality of one's sleep.*

Supplement Sleep with Napping

Sleep scientist Sara Mednick points out that naps can add back to the sleep you are deprived of, as well as enhance productivity even if you have enough nocturnal sleep, (*Napping Your Way to the Top*).

This gives hope to everyone who can't get in a long sleep time during the week. Use naps to supplement your sleeping.

The extra elements such as nutrition, optimal rest and recovery, and adequate sleep play important roles in getting the best benefits possible from Sprint 8. Eating clean, drinking plenty of water, avoiding refined sugar after Sprint 8, getting 20-30 grams of quality protein after training, planning for sufficient rest between workouts, and getting adequate sleep will maximize your Sprint 8 training.

Strengthen Your Base -- Your Feet

Your core is very important, and there are hundreds of articles and books about this topic. You are clearly working your core with Sprint 8 because cardio sprinting with all-out, sprint-intensity effort actually forces you to recruit all of the core muscle groups. Typically core is considered your abs, internal and external obliques, lower back, glutes, hip flexors and hip extensors.

Your core is extremely important, but **don't forget your base.** Your base -- your legs and especially your feet -- are equally important, but frequently neglected.

My book, *Ready, Set, Go! Fitness* has 100 pages of information on strength training and E-Lifting technique, which is to strength training what Sprint 8 is to cardio -- it's a time efficient method to work all three *muscle-fiber types* during strength training. While strength training isn't the focus of this book, I want to add an important strength training tip. Strengthen your core and your base.

For most of us, we live life on concrete. As human beings, we adapt by spending $21 billion a year on cushioned shoes with slightly elevated heels so our backs don't hurt when pounding the payment. We need these shoes. But at the same time, there is a downside for our cushioned shoes.

Wearing these wonderfully cushioned shoes makes our feet weak and the achilles tendon and the biceps femoris (in the hamstrings muscle group) abnormally tight. I'm not saying to throw out your comfortable shoes. But I am saying, you need to add some simple training to strengthen your feet and stretch the hamstrings, achilles and calves after doing Sprint 8.

Leg presses not only work your quads, glutes and hamstrings, but you should notice that the bottom-of-your-feet burn like crazy during the last few reps. This means that you have recruited your plantar tendons, and they are being worked during this exercise to the point they are burning. This is positive. You are making them stronger. When your plantar tendons burn during leg presses and during some jumping drills, this means you are creating micro-fiber tears in the plantar tendons. When you sleep, they will heal back stronger.

Reverse calf raises will work your shin-splint muscles, the tibialis. This exercise will also work the ligaments in the top of your feet at the same time to comprehensively strengthen your feet.

Reverse calf raises are simple to do. With an arm holding on for balance, stand on a step -- weight on your heels with mid-foot and toes hanging off the step. While keeping your knees locked and straight, lower and raise your toes as far as possible at a good pace. Pay close attention that your knees stay straight and locked and only your ankles are moving (as shown).

Reverse Calf Raises

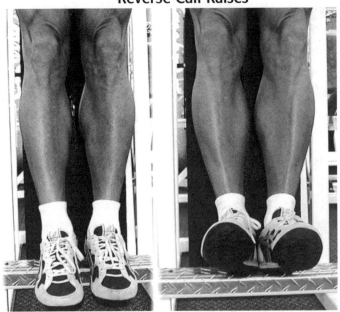

Sometimes it is helpful to slightly bend at the waist (like a banana), but keep your knees straight and locked. Only have your ankles move your toes up-and-down at a moderate pace -- until they fail -- and you can't do any more.

Don't stop because of the tibialis muscles burn. The burning is a built in barometer telling you, *now the exercise is productive.*

You are only doing this once-a-week, so push the intensity and stop when the muscles slow to the point they are barely moving.

You should feel the burn in the shin-splint (tibialis) muscles and this means you are clearly working this muscle group. At the same time, you are also working the ligaments in the top of your feet. Since these are ligaments, they don't have receptors for lactic acid like muscles do, but they are being worked nevertheless. They will get stronger when you sleep.

I recommend doing one set to failure once-a-week. If you do this correctly, one set of reverse calf raises to failure and try to walk immediately afterwards, it will feel like your feet aren't connected to your body for a few moments. Don't worry, the feeling will come back.

Case Study, Elizabeth Smith

Elizabeth Smith experienced great results during the first eight-weeks of the Sprint 8 Challenge. She continued with the Sprint 8 Protocol and continues to receive the benefits.

Elizabeth continued to do Sprint 8 three-times-a-week. Eighteen months later, she was 90 pounds lighter. Her body fat fell from 44 percent to 26 percent. Her HDL (good) cholesterol improved by 55 points. And her LDL (bad) cholesterol dropped from 102 to 72. Elizabeth's triglycerides fell from a very high 130 to a very low 35.

Elizabeth Smith used the Sprint 8 Protocol as a tool to completely change her health.

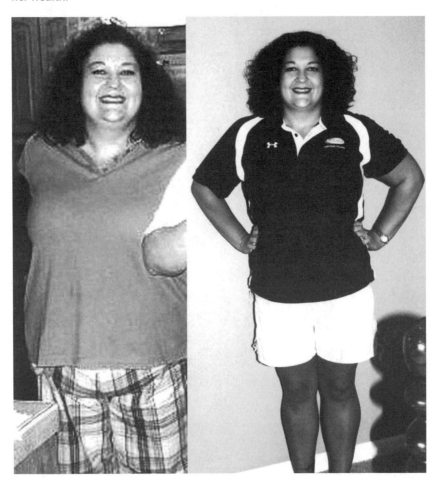

Conclusion

We have seen evidence that Sprint 8 may just be the magic formula everyone seems to be looking for in order to fight the outcomes of a sedentary lifestyle. Sprint 8 is the perfect tool for people to use today, even in this fast-food, sugar-hidden-in-everything world to get fit and stay fit.

Everyone is time crunched. Sprint 8 makes it work. All you need is 20 minutes, three-times-a-week and the willingness and motivation to be bulldog tough for two reps. Not all eight reps, but two reps the right way is how to start Sprint 8.

Begin with two 30-second cardio sprint reps on a cardio machine with 90 seconds of active recovery (after a two to three-minute warm-up). Don't feel duty bound to do two reps this time and three reps the next. Take your time adding reps. Listen to your body. You will know when it's time to add the next rep. Slowly and progressively build up to all eight reps.

Is Sprint 8 The Perfect Fitness Solution?

When I wrote the first edition of *Ready, Set, Go! Fitness,* the four growth hormone release benchmarks served as the main driver of the process to create the Sprint 8 Cardio Protocol. It's my belief that the body itself is telling us exactly how to exercise the best way for the best results. The huge release exercise-induced growth hormone is that barometer -- and this is what we should go by.

As we have seen throughout the book, exercise-induced growth hormone does many wonderful things for the body. Distinguished researcher, Dr. Thomas C. Welbourne says it should be called the *Fitness Hormone.* But there are many more things happening inside the body and the brain than just the release of growth hormone.

Growth hormone, however, is the barometer that should measure the effectiveness of exercise. This thinking originated from Dr. Richard Godfrey, and I want to give him credit for his revolutionary, out-of-box thinking.

Numerous new studies year-after-year unveil more and more affirmation that Sprint 8 should be in every exercise plan. We need to recruit and work *all three muscle-fiber types* and not just try to work higher in a HRT colored zone for longer than the last time. This method will increase exercise intensity, but it won't come close to what sprint-intensity cardio will do for you.

Interval Training Exercise Could be a Fountain of Youth is the title of an article written by Susan Scutti for CNN. She interviewed and reported on a major new study published in the *Journal Cell Metabolism*. Dr. Sreekumaran Nair, senior author of the study and researcher at Mayo Clinic was quoted in the article:

> *High-intensity interval training (HIIT), in particular, is highly efficient when it comes to **reversing many age-related changes**,* (Scutti, Susan, (2017) *http://www.cnn.com/2017/03/07/health/interval-training-exercise-cellular-aging-study/index.html.* Wed March 8, 2017).

The three-days-a-week, 12-week study had 36 men and 36 women from two age groups. The *young group* was age 18-30. The *older group* was 65-80 years old. Subjects were placed into three different exercise programs; high-intensity interval biking, strength training with weights, and a combined group of strength training and lower-intensity interval training five days-a-week. Biopsies of muscle were obtained to compare the changes at the cellular level in their muscle cells vs sedentary individuals. The amount of lean muscle mass and insulin sensitivity was also measured.

The researchers learned that high-intensity interval training (HIIT) improved insulin sensitivity, which reduces the risk of diabetes in all ages. While strength training was effective at building muscle mass, it was the high-intensity interval training that yielded the greatest benefits at the cellular level.

Both groups, ***young and old, had significant improvements with HIIT. The young interval training group achieved a 49% increase in mitochondria capacity. The older group achieved a huge 69% increase***. (Robinson, MM. (2017) *Enhanced Protein Translation Underlies Improved Metabolic and Physical Adaptations to Different Exercise Training Modes in Young and Old Humans.* Cell Metab. 2017 Mar 7;25(3):581-592. doi: 10.1016/j.cmet.2017.02.009).

In an interview with *Science Daily*, Dr. Nair concluded;

> Based on everything we know, there's no substitute for these exercise programs when it comes to delaying the aging process. **These things we are seeing cannot be done by any medicine,** *(https://www.sciencedaily.com/releases/2017/03/170307155214.htm)*

Susan Scutti also reported on Dr. Nair's conclusions;

> *Analyzing the muscle biopsies, the researchers discovered that exercise boosts cellular production of mitochondrial proteins and the proteins responsible for muscle growth.*
>
> *"Exercise training, especially high intensity interval training, enhanced the machinery (ribosomes) to produce proteins, increased the production of proteins and enhanced protein abundance in muscle," Nair said. He said the results also showed that "the substantial increase in mitochondrial function that occurred, especially in the older people, is due to increase in protein abundance of muscle." In some cases, the **high-intensity regimen actually seemed to reverse the age-related decline in both mitochondrial function and muscle-building proteins.***
>
> *Exercise's ability to transform mitochondria could explain why it benefits our health in so many different ways, according to the authors. Muscle cells, like brain and heart cells, are unusual in that they divide only rarely compared with most cells in the body. Because muscle, brain and heart cells do wear out yet are not easily replaced, the function of all three of these tissues are known to decline with age, noted Nair.*
>
> ***If exercise restores or prevents deterioration of mitochondria and ribosomes in muscle cells, exercise possibly performs the same magic in other tissues, too.** And, although it is important simply to understand how exercise impacts the mechanics of cells, these insights may also allow researchers "to develop targeted drugs to achieve some of the benefits that we derive from the exercise in people who cannot exercise," Nair said.* (Scutti, Susan (2017), CNN. *http://www.cnn.com/2017/03/07/health/interval-training-exercise-cellular-aging-study/index.html).*

While this research is very exciting and affirms the premise of my first book *Ready, Set, Go! Fitness*, initially written in 1999. In many respects, Dr. Nair's study and the other studies cited in this book offers a very inexpensive preventative cure for many illnesses and diseases, including a possible positive impact on cancer prevention.

Every week there seems to be a major news story about the high cost of healthcare and how this one issue is killing the US financially. The financial cure for Medicare and Medicaid really is simple. Keep people out of the hospital because they are healthy, inspired, productive, and they don't need to use the sickcare system.

Sorry to be so simplistic. But if sickcare utilization went down by 20 percent, the US financial problems are close to resolved. There would be lots of money to pay off the debt service -- if we could give people a 20 minute, three-days-a-week, realistic program.

I agree with Dr. Nair and I like the thought of creating a drug to replicate the benefits of what the Sprint 8 Protocol can do *for people who can't exercise*. We actually have this today, it's injectable growth hormone. The purpose of this book is to prove there is a better way to increase growth hormone. Naturally! You can do this naturally with the Sprint 8 Cardio Protocol.

As presented in Chapter 1 *New Tools for a New You,* and throughout this book, the body is screaming at us through research telling us exactly how to exercise to get the best results in the shortest amount of time.

Very few people exercise more than moderate intensity, at best. When new and so-called innovative fitness programs hit the marketplace, they are still using old world thinking of trying to step-it-up just enough to get the heart rate up with a ground-based exercise, like you are going to get extra credit for doing something on the ground -- your body could care less. Your body doesn't care if it's done on the ground with body weight, with bands, with cables, with barbells, with dumbbells, or on a machine. Your body doesn't care. Your body cares about micro-fiber tears in the muscle fiber and a couple of days sleep with good nutrition along the way.

If you notice, most people in fitness centers are moving along at a slow to moderate pace, working the body, but not really pushing it hard. When the exercise gets hard and the muscles start burning, they stop as if they have accomplished the goal. When, in real life -- they quit when the warm up was over.

Intense training is tough to do. It's hard. However, it is vigorous, intense training that opens the doors to substantial, positive change to the body. Improved health, more energy, more muscle, less body fat are the things that most people want. And you can have them.

Start Sprint 8 Safely

In the beginning of this book, you read about the purpose -- I want to give you *New Tools for a New You*. New tools with the motivation from study after study to provide motivation for you to safely add sprint-cardio and change your life. The tools are the different ways to do the Sprint 8 Cardio Protocol. The science on top of science should give you the motivational base to call on as you begin the Sprint 8.

While I hope you will take the eight-week Sprint 8 Challenge (after getting your physician to clear you for anaerobic exercise), this book isn't about the eight-week Sprint 8 test drive.

My goal is simple. I want you to start Sprint 8 safely and continue the Sprint 8, three-days-a-week for a life time. My wish is for you to enjoy good health, superior fitness and revved up energy for an exciting life -- for the rest of your life.

Sprint 8 is hard. There's nothing harder. But it works. And it works in 20 minutes, three-days-a-week. For motivation to stick with the plan, it will be helpful to have your body fat and cholesterol tested before starting the Sprint 8 so you can track your success with important health measures.

As I said in the beginning of this book, it's always a great idea to have your physician clear you for anaerobic exercise before starting sprint cardio, or any new exercise program. If you have been sedentary, this is really important. The goal is to strengthen your heart muscle, not harm it. If someone has clogged arteries, and does high-intensity exercise and blood can't flow, this can do damage. And this is the exactly the opposite of what Sprint 8 is about.

Heart rate zones

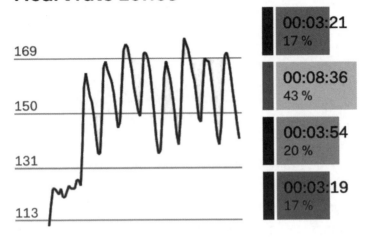

Sprint 8 heart muscle performance from Jason Parker

Unless you are a sprinter, you will be somewhat new to sprint cardio. You will be using *fast-muscle fiber* that may not have been recruited and worked in a few years. You will be pushing your muscles, tendons, ligaments and joints at higher speeds than they have experienced in a few years -- maybe even higher speeds than they have ever experienced before. This is positive, but the foundation for sprint-cardio intensity needs to be built safely.

It's important to *not* jump-the-gun and false start with a pulled hamstring trying to sprint run the Sprint 8. It's a good idea to start with a fitness center or home cardio unit to *get the feel* for Sprint 8. Please use the progressive, *Ramp Up Protocol* in Chapter 8 for sprint running on a track and resist the temptation to air-out the last rep full speed for several weeks. The hamstrings need 6 to 8 weeks of progressively building the *fast-muscle fiber* to safety handle full-speed sprint running.

When I'm asked, *is sprint-intensity cardio the fountain of youth?* I typically answer, there is nothing you can do to change your geological age, but when it comes to biological aging, Sprint 8 significantly increases growth hormone, which is being called the anti-aging hormone by many experts today.

Sprint 8 Cardio conditions both the anaerobic and aerobic processes of the heart muscle. It strengthens all *three muscle fiber types*, and it reduces body fat, builds muscle, and thickens skin, which is reported to make people appear younger and healthier. Some estimates are people, especially middle-age women, appear to be as much as 20 years younger.

Sprint 8 doubles the amount of energy-producing mitochondria and the extra energy boost makes people feel younger. Sprint 8 doubles the feel-good and get-motivated dopamine neurotransmitter in the brain. And sprint-intensity cardio preserves the length of your telomeres that are shown to be related with health and longevity.

Are you ready to take the eight week Sprint 8 Challenge?

Martha Bejarano and Boris Schatalow met in the Sprint 8 Challenge Class (see dopamine pp. 89-91).
Martha's amazing results are reported on pages 53-54. Boris gained 2 pounds of muscle, cut his body fat from 29.6 to 17.9 percent, and lost 23 pounds.

Frequently Asked Questions

How do I preload before a Sprint 8 workout for the best results?
As discussed in Chapter 9, page 140, *preload before* Sprint 8 may help get you
get better results:

L-glutamine -- 2 grams
Banana -- to reduce exercise-induced hypoglycemia
Dark Chocolate 85% Cocoa -- one square
(*Epicatechin supports mitochondria health*)

What is Sprint 8? Sprint 8 is the most effective and time-efficient cardio workout you can do. It only takes 20 minutes, three-days-a-week, and it is scientifically proven to work. The high-intensity portion of this exercise program amounts to four minutes per workout. That's only 12 minutes of high-intensity per week. Sprint 8 releases exercise-induced growth hormone, which is shown to reduce body fat, increase lean muscle, and improve energy.

What is Growth Hormone? Growth hormone, sometimes called human growth hormone and HGH, is a product of the pituitary gland, the master gland of the body. This hormone promotes linear growth in children and adolescents. After the body stops growing taller, the levels of growth hormone begin to decline. Dr. T.C. Welbourne calls it the *Fitness Hormone* because it reduces body fat and adds lean muscle.

What is somatopause? Somatopause is a medical term for loss of muscle, energy decline and wrinkled skin experienced in middle age. Somatopause may be alleviated through growth hormone injections to artificially increase growth hormone levels, or through anaerobic exercise, which naturally increases growth hormone levels.

How can I use Sprint 8 to train for endurance events? Sprint 8 improves performance at the cellular level by producing more ATP energy-producing mitochondria. This can double endurance capacity in as little as two weeks.

What are telomeres? Telomeres are found on the ends of chromosomes and they protect our DNA from damage. The American Heart Association has linked the presence of long telomeres with health, youth, and older adults with healthy lifestyles. AHA also found short telomeres to be associated with obesity, weight gain and diabetes. Telomere length is shown to be preserved in healthy older adults who perform maximum-intensity exercise.

Am I too old to do the Sprint 8 program? Technically, the older you get, the more beneficial the Sprint 8 Protocol becomes. It's specifically designed to combat the symptoms of aging people begin to experience during their mid-30s.

What is anaerobic exercise? Anaerobic exercise is high-intensity, short-duration exercise that builds strength, speed and endurance through mitochondria biogenesis (the body creating more mitochondria to handle increased demands for energy). Anaerobic exercise is a natural, healthy way to produce exercise-induced growth hormone.

What are mitochondria, and why are they important? Mitochondria are microscopic organelles in cells. They play an important role in creating energy for the body. The body takes nutrition and oxygen through mitochondria to create more energy (ATP). High-intensity exercise over an eight-week period can as much as double your mitochondria count and triple their energy output.

What areas of my body does Sprint 8 work? The body consists of three *muscle-fiber types* (*slow, fast, super-fast muscle cells*), three energy systems and two processes of the heart muscle. Sprint 8 works them all. When you do a Sprint 8 workout, your brain determines that your slow-twitch muscle fiber is inadequate to keep up. Your brain then recruits *fast and super-fast muscle* to propel the movement faster. Working muscle fiber with exercise creates microtrauma in the muscle cells that heal back bigger and stronger when we sleep.

What are fast muscle fibers? *Fast-muscle fiber* make up approximately 50 percent of muscle composition for the average person. Strengthening *fast (IIa) and super-fast (IIx) muscle fiber* is important for achieving the many benefits of anaerobic exercise.

Why is Sprint 8 more effective than working out with less intensity for a longer time period? Low-intensity training does not recruit *fast-twitch muscle fiber* needed to increase exercise-induced growth hormone. Sprint cardio can burn body fat for two full hours and longer after the workout is complete.

How is Sprint 8 different from any other interval cardio program? Sprint 8 requires your absolute *maximum intensity* and is more demanding than any other form of exercise. Sprint 8 is more efficient than interval training. Matrix Fitness and Vision Fitness® cardio machines are specifically manufactured to withstand the extra demand sprint-intensity cardio places on exercise equipment.

Can I do additional exercise to supplement a Sprint 8 workout? Yes. You should add the 10-minute stretching program after Sprint 8 when your muscles are warm. Strength training is important for everyone especially women, to prevent muscle and bone loss. There are comprehensive strategic fitness plans for five different fitness levels in *Ready, Set, Go! Fitness for Time-Crunched Adults.* There are complete strength training plans, and Chapter 6 covers the stretching routine, which generally gets an average of four inches of measurable flexibility in four weeks -- *www.readysetgofitness.com*

How do I determine which level to start? You should begin with two cardio sprint reps on resistance level 2 to 5. If the 30-second cardio sprint is not difficult to finish, increase the intensity to a higher resistance level, and go faster. It generally takes two or three workouts to get the feel for Sprint 8.

On a bike or elliptical, how do I determine speed? You should go as fast as your *fast-muscle fiber* will allow during the 30-second cardio sprint. Watch your RPMs, or *Sweat Score* on Matrix Fitness cardio units as a guide of your velocity.

Can I do Sprint 8 everyday? Although people can tolerate *slow-muscle fiber* exercise several days-in-a-row, fast-fiber work with Sprint 8 is much more demanding and research suggests *fast-muscle fiber* needs 48 hours to totally heal, so every other day is best for Sprint 8.

How do I know if I'm releasing growth hormone during & after the workout? Doing the all-out cardio sprints that are part of the Sprint 8 Protocol is the best insurance since the program was created specifically to release exercise-induced growth hormone.

Does growth hormone cause bigger muscles and a bulkier physique? Women do not have to worry about a bulky physique unless they are injecting testosterone. Adding some lean muscle will increase the resting metabolism, which in turn burns more body fat.

Could taking supplements could interfere with my medication? Yes, the Website *www.medlineplus.gov* has helpful resources on checking drug interactions with nutrition supplements.

Where is growth hormone produced in my body? Growth hormone is stored in the pituitary gland until it is released into the blood stream. The brain tells the hypothalamus gland that sits above the pituitary when to release growth hormone into the body. The hypothalamus gland controls the number of growth hormone pulse releases and the amount that is released in each pulse. The largest releases of growth hormone are during deep sleep and during sprint-intensity cardio.

What are METs? *Metabolic Equivalent Tasks* can be seen on many pieces of cardio and on Matrix Fitness cardio units. A MET number is similar to watts on cardio units as they both measure the combination of resistance and the velocity of movement. METs produces an easier number for most people to relate to during the hard 30-second cardio sprint, unless you are a cyclist and experienced in reading watts. The best measurement system for Sprint 8 is the *Sweat Score.*

What is Sweat Score? The *Sweat Score* measurement system was created by Matrix Fitness for Sprint 8 that is based on Joules for an easy-to-relate to system based on a true measurement of power. Sweat Score (joules) is a quantifiable measure of the amount of energy being generated during each Sprint 8 cardio sprint.

Glossary

Aerobic Exercise - Exercise that allows your body to consistently replenish its need for oxygen during fitness training. It is performed at a low to moderate intensity for 20 to 30 minutes. Aerobic exercise is frequently called *cardio* and is used to build endurance and cardiovascular conditioning.

Amino Acids - Building blocks of protein, which builds and repairs the body.

Anabolic - Growth oriented. The building-up cycle of the human body. Anabolic is opposed to catabolic, the breaking-down of body tissue.

Anaerobic Exercise - Brief, fast, high-intensity exercise that uses oxygen faster than the body can replenish it. Anaerobic exercise is a natural way to produce growth hormone, which reduces wrinkles, increases energy, reduces body fat and builds lean muscle.

Antioxidants - Compounds that lessen tissue oxidation and damage to the body. Small compounds assist in controlling potentially damaging free radical cells.

ATP - A high-energy molecule that provides energy to the body at the cellular level. ATP transports chemical energy within cells for metabolism.

Atrophy - The loss and wasting of muscle due to inactivity.

Carbs / Carbohydrates – Nutrients supplying energy to the body expressed as *simple* (sugar), and *complex* (grains).

Catecholamines – Natural hormones produced by the body (adrenaline and norepinephrine). The body's release of *Catecholamines* during exercise is a growth hormone release benchmark.

Concentric - The lifting phase when the muscle shortens. The *positive* movement of an exercise opposed to the *negative* eccentric lengthening phase.

Contraction – Movement of a muscle that results in shortening a muscle to push or pull resistance.

Cool down – The gradual slowing down of heart rate and body temperature that occurs between exercise and normal functioning of the body.

Dehydration – Losing too much body fluid during training. This can become dangerous if the body does not get replenished with fluid during training. Dehydration interferes with the release of growth hormone during exercise.

Dorsiflexion - The ankle bending the foot upward during running to gain power from increased ankle action. Opposite of plantarflexion (toe/foot down).

Dopamine - Dopamine is classified as a catecholamine (a class of molecules that serve as neurotransmitters and hormones). In the brain, dopamine functions as a neurotransmitter—a chemical released by neurons (nerve cells) to send signals to other nerve cells.

Eccentric - The lowering phase when the muscle lengthens. The *negative* movement of an exercise. Example, bench press has two phases: eccentric and concentric. Lowering the weight toward your chest is the eccentric phase or muscle-lengthening *negative* motion. Lifting the weight back up is the concentric, or muscle-shortening phase.

Endorphins – A natural chemical released by the body during training. Endorphins are released by the pituitary gland and act on the nervous system to reduce sensitivity to pain.

Endurance – The ability to perform exercise for an extended period.

Exercise – Prescribed body movements intended to develop the body by working muscle groups.

Fat – An essential nutrient that is a source of energy for the body.

Fast-twitch muscle fibers - Muscle fibers make up half of muscle composition for the average person. Building fast (IIa) and super-fast (IIx) muscle fibers are the key to anaerobic exercise, which can be built through sprint cardio training.

Fatigue - The point in exercise where the muscle begins to weaken.

Flexibility – The ability of muscle and connective tissue attached to joints to move in a full range of motion. Flexibility is increased through stretching.

Glucose – A *simple* sugar used by the body for energy.

Glutamine - Amino acid shown effective in increasing growth hormone.

Glycogen – Substance formed by carbohydrates. Stored in the body as energy.

Growth Hormone (GH) – A hormone produced by the pituitary gland responsible for promoting and regulating muscle and tissue growth, regulating carbohydrates and fat metabolism, and controlling other vital glands.

HDL Cholesterol - High-density lipoprotein. Also known as *good* cholesterol because it has scavenger abilities to remove fats in the blood.

Hypoglycemia – low blood sugar.

Intensity - The amount of stress on the body while performing an exercise. Typically classified as low, moderate, and high intensity, however, this book has one higher level. The highest level of exercise intensity is *sprint intensity*.

Lactic Acid – During exercise sugar is broken down into different chemicals to produce energy for muscles to continue moving. When you perform sprint-intensity cardio, the body can't get all the oxygen it needs to keep moving fast, and a chemical called lactic acid begins to accumulate in the muscles and spill into the bloodstream.

LDL Cholesterol - Low-density lipoprotein. Sometimes called *bad* cholesterol due to its negative impact on the cardiovascular system when out of balance with HDL cholesterol.

Metabolism - The chemical reactions that occur in the body. *Metabolic rate* is the rate at which the body utilizes energy. Exercise increases metabolic rate.

Mitochondria - Mitochondria are powerhouses of the cell. They take in nutrients, break them down, and create energy rich molecules for the cell called ATP.

Muscle Tone – The condition of muscle that appears healthy and firm.

Nutrients – Nourishment for the body. Macro nutrients are carbohydrates, protein, fat and water. Micro nutrients are vitamins and minerals. *Essential nutrients* must be obtained from the diet.

Obesity – Over 30 percent body fat.

Periodization – A training method that varies training to prepare an athlete to achieve *peak* performance at the prescribed time.

Plateau – The halting or leveling off of gains in fitness and training.

Protein – Protein is one of three micronutrients: protein, fats and carbohydrates that provide calories for energy. Amino acids are the building blocks of different proteins, and proteins are the building blocks of muscle mass, according to the National Institutes of Health (NIH).

Recovery – Recovery has several meanings in exercise and fitness.
(1) Recovery is the brief period between sets generally lasting 30-90 seconds.
(2) Recovery is the period immediately following a training session that typically lasts 20 -30 minutes.
(3) Total recovery from exercise can take 24 and up to 48 hours for the microtrauma in muscles to completely heal.

Repetition (Rep) - One complete movement of an exercise.

Resistance – The amount of weight or force used in an exercise.

Routine – The configuration of exercises - sets and reps utilized in strength and fitness training.

Set – A series of repetitions. Example: *2 sets of 10 repetitions.*

Somatopause – A physical condition characterized by high insulin levels, low growth hormone, which leads to weight gain, increased body fat, obesity, high cholesterol, and heart disease. Sometimes called *The middle-age spread.*

Somatostatin – A hormone that inhibits the release of growth hormone.

Strength training – Exercise to increase strength; weight lifting.

Synergistic – Parts working together and producing more together than the individual parts would produce alone.

Technique – The form utilized in performing the biomechanics of an exercise.

Telomeres -- Telomeres are found on the ends of chromosomes. They protect cells. Long telomeres are associated with health and longevity. Short telomeres are associated obesity, weight gain and poor health. Telomere length is preserved in healthy, older adults who perform maximum-intensity anaerobic exercise.

Vitamin D – Vitamin D is a fat-soluble vitamin naturally present in very few foods. People can't get the right amount of Vitamin D your body needs from food and Vitamin D^3 supplements are typically necessary. Vitamin D^3 is the recommended form of vitamin D since this is the natural form of vitamin D your body makes from sunlight. Vitamin D is also classified as a hormone because it has other roles in the body -- including modulation of cell growth, neuromuscular and immune function, and reduction of inflammation.

Warm-up – Slow and mild exercise that seeks to raise body temperature by one degree prior to fitness training.

References

Ahmaidi, (1998). "Effects of interval training at ventilatory thresholds on clinical and cardiorespiratory responses in elderly humans." Eur J Appl Physiol Occup Physiol. Jul;78(2):170-6.).

Ames, BN. (2001). "DNA damage from micro nutrient deficiencies is likely to be a major cause of cancer." Mutat Res. Apr 18;475(1-2):7-20. PMID: 11205149.

Antonio, (2000). "Effects of exercise training and amino-acid supplementation on body composition and physical performance in untrained women." Nutrition. Nov-Dec;16(11-12):1043-6. PMID: 11118822.

Atalay, Sen. (1999). "Physical exercise and antioxidant defenses in the heart." Ann N Y Sci. Jun30;874:169-77. PMID: 10415530.

Bayat, A. (2011). "Practical model of low-volume high-intensity interval training induces performance and metabolic adaptations that resemble 'all-out' sprint interval training." Sports Sci Med. 2011 Sep 1;10(3):571-6. 2011).

Bell (2000). "Effect of concurrent strengthand endurance training on skeletal muscle properties and hormone concentrations in humans." EurJ Appl Physiol. Mar;81(5):418).

Bemben DA,(2000). "Musculoskeletal responses to high- and low–intensity resistance training in early postmenopausal women." Med Sci Sports Exerc. Nov;32(11):1949).

Bewaerets, Moorkens, Abs. (1998). "Secretion of growth hormone in patientswith chronic fatigue syndrome." Growth Hormone IGF Res, April 8, Suppl B: 127-9).

Biswas, A. (2015). "A Sedentary Time and Its Association With Risk for Disease Incidence, Mortality, and Hospitalization in Adults: A Systematic Review and Meta-analysis."Annuals of Internal Medicine, Vol 162, No. 2, Jan. 20.

Boecker H, (2008). "The runner's high: opioidergic mechanisms in the human brain. Cerebral cortex" (New York, N.Y. : 1991), 18 (11), 2523-31 PMID: 18296435)

Booth, Gordon, Carlson, Hamilton. (2000). "Waging war on modern chronic diseases: primary prevention through exercise biology. J Appl Physiol. Feb;88(2):774-87).

Borst, (2001). "Effects of resistance training on insulin-like growth factor-1 and IGF binding proteins." Med Sci Sports Exerc. Apr;33(4):648-653).

Bruls, Crasson, Van Reeth, Legros. (2000). "Melatonin. II. Physiological and therapeutic effects." Rev Med Liege. Sept;55(9):862-70. PMID: 11105602.

Burgomaster KA,,Gibala MJ. (2005). Si x sessions of sprint interval training increases muscle capacity in humans. 2005, J Appl Physiol.

Burt, D. (2012)."Targeting exercise-induced growth hormone release: A novel approach to fighting obesity by substantially increasing endogenous GH serum levels naturally."KDMC, Brookhaven, MS, http://www.readysetgofitness.com/obesity_research2.shtml.

Calabresi,(1996). "Somatostatin infusion suppresses GH secretory burst frequency and mass in normal men." American Journal of Physiology. Jun;270(6 Pt1):E975-9).

Cappon, Ipp, Brasel, Cooper. (1993). "Acute effects of high fats and high glucose meals on the growth hormone response to exercise." J Clin Endocrinol Metab. Jun;76(6):1418-22. PMID: 8501145.

Casabiell, (1999). "Growth hormone secretagogues: the clinical future." Horm Res 1999;51 Suppl 3:29-33. National Library of Science, PubMed abstract: 10592441.

Centers for Disease Control and Prevention. (2000). "CDC: Diabetes, obesity becoming epidemic." AP News. January 25,2001. www.Healthcentral.com.

Centers for Disease Control and Prevention. (2000). "Diabetes, A SeriousPublic Health Problem, AT-A-GLANCE 2000." Diabetes Public Health Resource).

Chein, Vogt, Terry. (1999). "Clinical experiences using a low-dose, high frequency human growth hormone treatment regimen." Journal of Advancement in Medicine. 12(3). www.drchein.com.

Christensen, (1984). "Characterization of growth hormone release in response to external heating. Comparison to exercise induced release." Acta Endocrinol. Nov;107(3): 295-301).

Chwalbinski-Moneta. (1996). "Threshold increases in plasma growth hormone in relation to plasma catecholamine and blood lactate concentration during progressive exercise in endurance-trained athletes." Eur J Appl Physiol Occup Physiol. 73(1-2):117-20).

Colao, Marzullo, Spiezia. (1999). "Effect of growth hormone and insulin like growth factor on prostate diseases: An ultrasonographic and endocrine study in Acromegaly, GH deficiency, and healthy subjects." J. Clinical Endocrinol Metab. 84:1986-91.

Colgan, Michael. (1993). Optimum Sports Nutrition, Your Competitive Edge. New York, NY. Advanced Research Press.

Corpas, Harman, Blackman. (1993). Human growth hormone and humanaging." Endocrinol Review, Feb; 14(1):20-39).

Cox, (1999). "Effect of aging on response to Exercise training in humans: skeletal muscle GLUT-4 and insulin sensitivity." J Applied Physiology. June;86(6):2019-25.

Cuneo, Salomon, Wiles, Sonksen. (1990). "Skeletal muscle performance in adults with growth hormone deficiency." Horm Res. 33 Suppl 4:66-60.PMID: 2245969.

Dall R, (2002). "Plasma ghrelin levels during exercise in healthy subjects and in growth hormone-deficient patients." Eur J Endocrinol. Jul;147(1):65-70).

D'Costa, (1993). The regulation and mechanism of Action of growth hormone and insulin-like growth factor 1 during normal aging." Journal of Reproductive Fertil Suppl:46:87-98).

Desaphy, (1998). "Partial recovery of skeletal muscle sodium channel properties in aged rats chronically treated with growth hormone or the GH secretagogue hexarelin." J Pharmacol Exp Ther. Aug;286(2):903-12).

Di Luigi, (2001). "Acute effect of physical exercise on serum insulin-like growth factor-binding protein 2 and 3 in healthy men: role of exercise linked growth hormone secretion." Int J Sports Med. Feb;22(2):103-110).

Di Luigi, (1999). "Acute amino Acids supplementation enhances pituitary responsiveness in athletics." Med Sci Sports Exerc. Dec;31(12):1748-54).

Dudley G (1982). "Influence of exercise intensity and duration on biochemical adaptations in skeletal muscle." J. Appl. Phsiol, 53, 844-850).

Dunstan, (2002) "High-Intensity resistance training improves glycemic control in older patients with type 2 diabetes." Diabetes Care, Oct;25(10):1729-36).

Dunkin, Ratini, (2014). *"Human Growth Hormone,"* Dec 30, 2014. *http://www.webmd.com/fitness-exercise/human-growth-hormone-hgh?page=2.*

Elias, (1997). "Effects of blood pH and blood lactate ongrowth hormone, prolactin, and gonadotropin release after acute exercise in male volunteers. Proc Soc Exp Biol Med. Feb;214(2):156-60. PMID: 9034133.

El-Khoury. (2000). "Twenty-four hour oral tracer studies with L-lysine at a low and intermediate lysine intake in healthy adults." Am J Clin Nutr. Jul;72(1):122-30).

Felsing, Brasel, Cooper. (1992). "Effect of low and high intensity exercise on circulating growth hormone in men. J Clin Endocrinol Metab. Jul;75(1):157-62. PMID: 1619005.

Field, (2001) "Impact of overweight on the risk of developing common chronic diseases during a 10-year period." Arch Intern Med. Jul 9;161(13):1581-6).

Fossel, M. T(2015). *The Telomerase Revolution: The Enzyme That Holds the Key to Human Aging...and Will Soon Lead to Longer, Healthier Lives* BenBella Books ,Dallas

Frewin, Frantz, Downey. (1976) "The effect of ambient temperature onrgowth hormone and prolactin response to exercise. Aust J Exp Biol Med Sci. Feb:54(1):97-101).

Gagnon D. (2014). "The effects of cold exposure on leukocytes, hormones and cytokines during acute exercise in humans." 2014 Oct 22;9(10).

Gaskill, Serfass. Bacharach, Kelly. (1999). "Responses to training in cross-country skiers." Med Sci Sports Exerc. Aug;31(8):1211-7. PMID: 10449026.

Gastin, PB. (2001). "Energy system interaction and relative contribution during maximal exercise." Sports Med 2001;31(10):725-41. PMID: 115478894.

Gibala. (2000),"Nutritional supplementation and resistance exercise: what is the evidence for enhanced skeletal muscle hypertrophy?" Can J Appl Physiol. Dec;25(6):524).

Gilbala, M. Burgomaster K, (2005). "Six sessions of sprint interval training increases muscle oxidative potential and cycle endurance capacity in humans."J Appl Physiol. Jun.

Gibney, Wallace, Spinks. (1999). "The effects of 10 years of recombinant growth hormone (GH) in adult GH-deficient patients." J Clin Endocrinol Metab. 84:2596-2602.

Gist N. (2014) "Sprint interval training effects on aerobic capacity: a systematic review and meta-analysis. Sports Med. 2014 Feb;44(2):269-79).

Godfrey, RJ. (2003) "The exercise-induced growth hormone response in athletes." Sports Medicine. 33(8):599-613).

Godfrey RJ, (2009). "The role of lactate in the exercise-induced human growth hormone response: evidence from McArdle disease." Br J Sports Med. 2009 Jul;43(7).

Goji, K. 1993). "Pulsatile characteristics of spontaneous growth hormone (GH) concentration profiles in boys evaluated by an ultrasensitive immunoradiometric assay: evidence for ultradian periodicity of GH secretion." J Clinical Endocrinology Metabolism. Mar;76(3):667-70.

Gordon, Kraemer, Vos, Lynch, Knuttgen. (1994). "Effect of acid-base on growthhormone response to acute high-intensity cycle exercise." J Appl Physiol. Feb;76(2):821-9).

Groussard, (2000). Free radical scavenging and antioxidant effects of lactate ion: an in vitro study." J Appl Physiol. Jul;89(1):169-75. PMID: 10904049.

Hansen, Stevens, Coast. (2001). "Exercise duration and mood state: how much is enough to feel better?" Health Psychol. Jul;29(4):267-75. PMID: 11515738

Hennessey, (2001). "Growth hormone administration and exercise effects on muscle fiber type and diameter in modeRatey frail older people." J AM Geriatr. Jul:49(7):852-8).

Holl (1991). "Thirty-second sampling of plasma growth hormone in man: correlation with sleep stages." Journal Clin endocrinol Metab. Apr;72(4):854-61. PMID: 2005213.

Holloszy, J. (1967). "Effects of Exercise on Mitochondrial Oxygen Uptake and Respiratory Enzyme Activity in Skeletal Muscle," J of Biological Chemistry, vol. 242(9), pp. 2278-2282.

Hurel (1999). "Relationship pf physical exercise and aging to growth hormone production." Clin Endocrinol (Oxf). Dec;51(6):687-91. PMID: 10619972.

Ignacio, DL. (2015). "Thyroid hormone and estrogen regulate exercise-induced growth hormone release." PLoS One. 2015 Apr 13;10(4):e0122556).

Izquierdo. (2001). Effects of strength training on muscle power and serum hormones in middle-aged and older men. J Appl Physiol. Abstract-A531-0. Jan. 29,2001.

Jakicic, (1999). "Effects of intermittent exercise and use of home exercise equipment adherence, weight loss, and fitness in overweight women: a random trial." JAMA. Oct 27;282(16):1554-60).

Jenkins. (1999). "Growth hormone and exercise." Clin Endocrinol (Oxf). Jun;50(6):683-9. PMID: 10468938.

Jesper, Anderson, Schjerling, Saltin. (2000). Muscles, Genes and Athletic Performance." Scientific American. Sept(1)48-55.

Jones, L.,(2008). "Active Dehydration Impairs Upper and Lower Body Anaerobic Muscular Power." J Strength & Conditioning Research. March 22 Active Dehydration.

Jubrias, (2001). "Large energetic adaptations of elderly muscle to resistance and endurance training. J Appl Physiol. Abstract: 8:0057A. Feb. 27, 2001.

Jurca R,(2004 Aug). "Associations of muscle strength and fitness with metabolic syndrome in men." Med Sci Sports Exer).

Kami. . (2000). "Melatonin treatment for circadian rhythm sleep disorders." Psychiatry Clin Neurosci. Jun;54(3):381-2. PMID: 11186123.

Kanaley, Weatherup-Dentes, Jaynes, Hartman. (1999). "Obesity attenuates the growth hormone response to exercise." J Clin Endocrinol Metab.Sept;84(9):3156-61.

Kanaley, Weltman, Pieper,Weltman, Hartman. (2001). "Cortisol and growth hormone response to exercise at different times of day." J Clin EndocrinolMetab. Jun;86(6):2881-9).

Kastello, Sothmann, Murthy. (1993). "Young and old subjects for aerobic capacity have similar noradrenergic responses to exercise." J Appl Physiol. Jan;74(1):49-54).

Kiernan,(2000). "Characteristics of successfuld ieters: an application of signal detection methodology." Ann Behav Med. Winter;20(1):1-6).

Kindermann (1982.) "Catecholamines, growth hormone, cortisol, insulin, and sex hormones in anaerobic and aerobic exercise. Eur J Appl Occup Physiol. 49(3):389-99).

Kostka, T. (2000). "Physio-pathologic aspects of aging—possible influence of physical training on physical fitness." Przegl Lek. 57(9):474-6. PMID: 11199868.

Kreider. (1999). "Dietary supplements and the promotion of muscle growth with resistance exercise." Sports Med. Feb;27(2):97-110. PMID: 10091274.

Krzywkowski, (2001). "Effects of glutamine supplementation on exercise-induced changes in lymphocyte function." Am J Physiol Cell Physiol. Oct;281(4):C1259-65).

Lanzi, (1999). "Elevated insulin levels contribute to the reduced growth hormone (GH) response to GH-releasing hormone in obese subjects." Metabolism, Sept;48(9):1152-6).

Larocca T.J. (2010). "Leukocyte telomere length is preserved with aging in endurance exercise-trained adults and related to maximal aerobic capacity." Department of Integrative Physiology, University of Colorado, Boulder. Mech Ageing Dev. Feb;13 1(2):165-7.

Leach, RE. (2000). "Aging and Physical activity." Orthopade. Nov;29(11):936-40. PMID: 11149278.

Lemura, (2000). "The effects of physical training on functional capacity in adults. Ages 46 to 90: a meta-analysis." J Sports Med Phy Fitness. Mar;40(1):1-10. PMID: 10822903.

Lemura, (2000). "The effects of physical training on functional capacity in adults. Ages 46 to 90: a meta-analysis." J Sports Med Phy Fitness. Mar;40(1):1-10).

Lieberman, Hoffman. (1997). "The somatopause: should growth hormone deficiency in older people be treated?" Clinical Geriatric Medicine. Nov:13(4):671-84).

Linden, D. (2012). "Exercise, pleasure and the brain Understanding the biology of "runner's high," Psychology Today, Apr 21.

(Llorens-Martin, (2009) *Mechanisms mediating brain plasticity: IGF1 and adult hippocampal neurogenesis. The Neuroscientist,* 15, 134-148).

Lugar, (1992). "Plasma growth hormone and prolactin responses to graded levels of acute exercise and to a lactate infusion. Neuroendocrinology. 56;112-117.

Lugar. (1988). "Acute exercise stimulates the rennin-angiotensin-aldosterone axis adaptive changes in runners." Horm Res. 30(1);5-9. PMID: 2851526.

Marcell, (1999). "Oral arginine does not stimulate basal or augment exercise-induced GH secretion in either young or old adults." Journal of Gerontology. A Bio Sci Med Sci. Aug 54(8):M395-9).

Marcinik (1991.) "Effects of strength training on lactate thresholds and endurance performance." Med Sci Sports Ex. Jun;23(6):739-43).

Marharam, Bauman, Kalman, Skolnik, Perle. (1999). "Masters athletes: factors affecting performance." Sports Med. Oct;28(4):273-85. PMID: 10565553.

McGuire, (2001). "A 30-year follow-up of the Dallas Bedrest and training Study: II. Effect of age on cardiovascular adaptation to exercise training. Circulation. Sept 18;104(12):1358-66).

Meckel, Y. (2011) "Hormonal and inflammatory responses to different types of sprint interval training." J Strength Cond Res. 2011 Aug;25(8):2161-9).

Medbo, Burgers. (1990). "Effect of training on the anaerobic capacity." Med Sci Sports Exerc. Aug;22(4):501-7. PMID: 2402211.

Medbo, Tabata. (1989). "Relative importance of aerobic and anaerobic energy release during short-lasting exhausting bicycle exercise." J Appl Physiol. Nov;67(5):1881-6).

Meirleir,(1986). "Beta-endorphin and ACTH levels in peripheral blood during and after aerobic and anaerobic exercise." Eur J Appl Physiol Occup Physiol. 55(1):5-8).

Mestrovi, T, (2015). "Telomeres and Cancer," Nov 19, News-Medical, http://www.news-medical.net/life-sciences/Telomeres-and-Cancer.aspx).

Mirkin, G. (2016). "How to Strengthen Your Heart," www.DrMirkin.com, http://drmirkin.com/public/ezine080705.html. "Collapse After Exercise."http://drmirkin.com/fitness/collapse.html

Momany, (1981). "Design, synthesis, and biological activity of peptides which release growth hormone in vitro." Endocrinology. Jan;108(1):31-9. PMID: 6109621.

Mujika, Chatard, Busso, Geyssant, Barale, Lacoste. (1995). "Effects of training on performance in competitive swimming." Can J Appl Physiol. Dec;20(4):395-406).

Mujika, Padilla, Ibanez, Izquierdo, Gorostiaga. (2000). "Creatine supplementation and sprint performance in soccer." Med Sci Sports Exerc. Feb;32(2):518-25).

Nalcakan GR. (2014). "The Effects of Sprint Interval vs. Continuous Endurance Training on Physiological And Metabolic Adaptations in Young Healthy Adults." J Hum Kinet. 2014 Dec 30;44:97-109.

Nevill M, (1996). "Growth hormone responses to treadmill sprinting in sprint- and endurance trained athletes." Eur J Appl Occup Physiol. 72(5-6):460-7).

Nicklas, (1995)."Testosterone, growth hormone and IGF-1 responses to Acute and chronic resistive exercise in man aged 55-70 years." Int Journal Sports Medicine, Oct;16(7):445-50).

Oldenburg, Ann. (2000). "The fountain of youth flows from a needle." *USA Today.* Nov. 14, 2000.

Oliver TD. (2015) "Endurance vs. interval sprint training and/or resistance training; impact on microvascular dysfunction in type 2 diabetes." Am J Physiol Heart Circ Physiol. 2015 Sep 25:ajpheart.00440.2015).

Ornish, D. (2015). "Lifestyle Changes May Lengthen Telomeres, A Measure of Cell Aging." The Lancet Oncology, Sept 16.

Panton, (2000). "Nutritional supplementation of the leucine metabolite beta-hydroxy-beta-methylbutyrate (hmb) during resistance training." Nutrition. Sep;16(9):734-9).

Parise, Yarasheski. (2000). "The utility of resistance training and amino acid supplementation for reversing age-associated decrements in muscle protein mass and function." Curr Opin Clin Nutr Metab Care. Nov 3;(6):489-95. PMID:11085836.

Pedersen. (2016 Feb) *Voluntary Running Suppresses Tumor Growth through Epinephrine- and IL-6-Dependent NK Cell Mobilization and Redistribution. Cell Metabolism*).

Peyreigne, Bouix, Fedou, Mercier. (2001). "Effect of hydration on exercise-induced growth hormone." Eur J Endocrinol. Sept;145(4):445-50. PMID: 115810003.

Pfeifer, Verhovec, Zizek. (1999). "Growth hormone treatment reverses earlyatherosclerotic changes in GH deficient adults." J Clin Endocrinol Metab. 84:453-457.

Pritzlaff, Wideman, Weltman, J., Abbott, Gutgesell, Hartman, Veldhuis, Weltman, A. (2000). "Catecholamine release, growth hormone secretion, and energy expenditure during exercise vs. recovery in men." J Appl Physiol. Sept;89(3):937-46. PMID: 10956336.

Pritzlaff, Wideman, Weltman, J., Abbott, Gutgesell, Hartman, Veldhuis, Weltman, A. (2000). "Impact of acute exercise intensity on pulsatile growth hormone release in men." J Appl Physiol. Aug;87(2):498-504. PMID: 10444604.

Rao, G. (2001). "Insulin resistance syndrome." Am Fam Physician. Mar 15;63(6):1159-63, 1165-6. PMID: 11277552.

Ratey, J. (2008). "SPARK, The New Revolutionary New Science of Exercise and the Brain." (Little Brown and Company.

Reaven, G. (2001). "Syndrome X." 1092-8464 Aug;31(4):323-332).

Rennie, MJ. (2001). "Grandad, it ain't what you eat, it depends when you eat it – that's how muscles grow!" J Physiol. Aug 15;535(Pt 1):2. PMID: 11507153.

Roberts, Wilson. (1999). "Effect of stretching duration on active and passiverange of motion in the lower extremity." Br J Sports Med. Aug;33(4):259-63. PMID: 10450481.

Robinson, Sloan, Arnold. (2001). "Use of niacin in the prevention and management of hyperlipidemia." Prog Cardiovasc Nurs. Winter;16(1):14-20. PMID: 11252872.

Rodriguez-Arnao, Jabbar, Fulcher, Besswer, Ross. (1999). "Effects of growth hormone replacement on physical performance and body composition in GH deficient adults." Clin Endocrinol (Oxf). Jul;51(1):53-60. PMID: 10468965.

Roemmich, Rogol. (1997). "Exercise and growth hormone: does one affect the other?" J Pediatr. Jul;131(1 Pt 2):5S75-80. PMID: 9255234.

Ronsen, Haug, Pedersen, Bahr. (2001). "Increased neuroendocrine response to a repeated bout of endurance exercise." Med Sci Sports Exerc. Apr;33(4):568-75).

Ross, Dagnone, Jones, Smith, Paddags, Hudson, Janssen, (2000). "Reduction In obesity and related comorbid conditions after diet-induced weight loss or exercise-induced weight loss in Men. A randomized, controlled trial." A Intern Med. Jul 18;188(2):92-103).

Rubin, Rita. (2001 May 15). "More people need cholesterol drugs." USA Today.)

Rudman, Daniel, and colleagues. (1990). "Effects of human growth hormone in men over 60 years old." New England Journal of Medicine, Volume, 323,July 5, 1990).

Ryan, (2001). "Insulin action after resistive training in insulin resistant older men and women." J Am Geriatr Soc. Mar;49(3):247-53).

Sanders, Chaturvedi, Hordinski. (1999). "Melatonin: aeromedical, toxicopharmacological, and analytical." J Anal Toxicol. May-Jun;23(3):159-67. PMID: 10369324.

Schilling. (2001). "Creatine supplementation and health variables: a retrospective study." Med Sci Sports Exerc. Feb;33(2):183-8. PMID: 11224803.

Sesso, Paffenbarger, Lee. (2000). "Physical activity and coronary disease in men: The Harvard Alumni Health Study." Circulation. Aug29;102(9):975-80. PMID: 10961960.

Silverman, (1996). "Hormonal responses to maximal and submaximal exercise in trained and untrained men of various ages. J Gerontol A Biol Med Sci. Jan;51(1):B30-7).

Sim, AJ. (2014). "High-intensity intermittent exercise attenuates ad-libitum energy intake." Int J Obes (Lond). 2014 Mar;38(3):417-22).

Sipila, (1997). "Effects of strength and endurance training on muscle fiber characteristics in elderly women. Clin Physiol. Sept;17(5):459-74).

Snibson,(2001) "Overexpressed growth hormone (GH) synergistically promotes carcinogen-initiated liver tumour growth by promoting cellular proliferation in emerging hepatocellular neoplasms in female and male GH-transgenic mice. Liver. Apr;21(2):149).

Sothern. (2000). "Safety, feasibility, and efficacy of a resistance training program in preadolescent obese children." Am J Med Sci. Jun;310(6):370-5. PMID: 10875292.

Sothern, (2000). "Safety, feasibility, and efficacy of a resistance training program in preadolescent obese children." Am J Med Sci. Jun;310(6):370-5. PMID: 10875292.

Sports Club Association Newsletter, International Health Racket. Nov. 2000.

Stokes (2002). "Growth Hormone responses to repeated maximal cycle ergometer exercise at different pedaling rates." J Appl Physiol 2992 Feb;92(2):602-8).

Stone, (1999). "Effects of in-season (5-weeks) creatine and pyruvate supplements on anaerobic performance and body composition in American football players." Int J Sport Nutr. Jun;9(2):146-65).

Stromme, Hostmark. (2000). "Physical activity, overweight and obesity." Tidsskr Nor Laegeforen. Nov 30;120(29):3578-3582. PMID: 11188389.

Suminski,(1997) "Acute effect of amino acid ingestion and resistance exercise on plasma growthhormone concentration in young men." Int Journal Sports Nutrition, March;7(1):48-60).

Sutton J, (1976). "Growth hormone in exercise: comparison of physiological and pharmacological stimuli." J Appl Physiol. 1976 Oct;41(4):523-7.

Sutton, Lazarus. (1976). "Growth hormone in exercise: comparison of physiological and pharmacological stimuli." J Appl Physiol. Oct;41(4):523-7. PMID: 985395.

Sutton, (2001). "A case-control study to investigate the relation between low and moderate levels of physical activity and osteoarthritis of the knee, Ann Rheum Dis. Aug;60(8):756-64).

Sytze, Smid, Niesink, Bolscher, Waasdorp, Dieguez, Casanueva, Koppeschaar. (2000). "Reduction of free fatty acids by acipimox enhances the growth hormone responses to GH-releasing peptide 2 in elderly men." J Clin Endocrinol Metab. Dec;85(12):4706-11).

Tabrizi, McIntryre, Quesnel, Howard. (2000). "Limited dorsiflexion predisposes to injuries of the ankle in children." J Bone Joint Surg Br. Nov;82(8):1103-6).

Takala, Ruokonen, Webster. (1999). "Increased mortality associated with growth hormone treatment in critically Ill adults." N Eng J Med 341:785-92.

Taylor, Bachman. (1999). "The effects of endurance training on muscle fiber types and enzyme activities." Can J Appl Physiol. Feb;24(1):41-53. PMID: 9916180.

Terry, (1976). "Antiserum to somatostatin prevents stress-induced inhibition of growth hormone secretion in the rat." Science. May 7;192(4239):565-7).

Thomas SG, (2003) *"Exercise training benefits growth hormone-deficient adults in the absence or presence of GH treatment."* J Clin Endocrinol Metab. 2003 Dec;88(12):5734-8).

Toogood, O'Neill, Shalet. (1996). "Beyond the somatopause: growth hormone deficiency in adults over the age of 60 years." J Clin Endocrinol Metabol. Feb; 81(2):460-5. National Library of Science, PubMed abstract: 8636250.

Toogood, O'Neill, Shalet. (1996). "Beyond the somatopause: growth hormone deficiency in adults over the age of 60 years." J Clin Endocrinol Metab. Feb; 81(2):460-5).

Toogood, Shalet. (1998). "Aging and growth hormone." Baillieres Clinical Endocrinology Metabolism, July: 12 (2):281-96).

Trappe, Costill, Thomas. (2000). "Effect of swim taper on whole muscle and single muscle fiber contractile properties." Med Sci Sports Exerc.Dec;32(12):48-56).

Van Buul-Offers, Kooijman. (1998) "The role of growth hormone and insulin-likegrowth factors in the immune system." Cell Mol Life Science, Oct; 54(10): 1083-94).

Van Cauter, Copinschi. (2000). "Interrelationships between growth hormone and sleep." Growth Horm IGF Res. Apr;10 Suppl B:S57-62. PMID: 10984255.

Van Cauter, (2000). "Age-related changes in slow wave and REM sleep and relationship with growth hormone and cortisol levels in healthy men." JAMA. Aug16;284(7):861-8).

Vance. (1996.) "Nutrition, body composition, physical activity and growth hormone secretion." J Pediatr Endocrinol Metab. Jun;9 Suppl 3:299-301. PMID: 8887174.

VanHelder, Casey, Radomski. (1987). "Regulation of growth hormone during exercise by oxygen demand and availability." Eur J Appl Physiol Occup Physiol. 56(6):628-32).

VanHelder, Goode, Radomski. (1984). "Effects of anaerobic and aerobic exercise of equal duration and work expenditure on plasma growth hormone levels."Eur J Appl Physiol Occup Physiol. 52(3):255-7. PMID: 6539675.

Vanhelder, (1985). "Hormonal and metabolic response to three types of exercise of equal duration and external work output."Eur J Appl Occup Physiol. 54(4):337-42).

Vanhelder, Radomski, Goode. (1984). "Growth hormone responses during intermittent weight lifting exercise in Men." Eur J Physiol Occup Physiol. 53(1):31-4).

Vigas,(2000). "Role of body temperature in exercise-induced growth hormone and prolactin release in non-trained and physically fit subjects. Endocr Regul.Dec;34(4):175).

Vincent G. (2015). "Changes in mitochondrial function and mitochondria associated protein expression in response to 2-weeks of high intensity interval training." Front Physiol. Feb 24;6:51).

Wahl P, (2013). "Effects of active vs. passive recovery during Wingate-based training on the acute hormonal, metabolic and psychological response." Growth Horm IGF Res. 2013 Dec;23(6):201-8).

Welbourne, TC. (2002). "Boost Your Growth Hormone Output Through Amino Acid Supplements," Dept. of Molecular Cellular Physiology, LSU Medical Center.

Welbourne, TC. (1995). "Increased plasma bicarbonate and growth hormoneafter an oral glutamine load." American Journal of Clinical Nutrition, Vol.61,1058-1061. National Library of Science, PubMed abstract: 7733028.

Weltman, Pritzlaff, Wideman, Blumer, Abbott, Hartman, Veldhuis. (2000). "Exercise-dependent growth hormone release is linked to markers of heightened central adrenergic outflow." J Appl Physiol. Aug;89(2):629-35.

Weltman, Weltman, Womack, Davis, Blumer, Gasser, Hartman. (1997). "Exercise training decreases the growth hormone (GH) response to acute constant-load exercise." Med Sci Sports Exer. May;29(5):660-76.

WHO (2015). "Physical Activity Fact sheet N°385" World Health Organization, Jan.

Wideman L, Weltman, Shah, Story, Veldhuis, Weltman A. (1999). "Effects of gender on exercise-induced growth hormone release." J Appl Physiol. Sept;87(3):1154-62).

Wideman, (2002). "Growth hormone Release during acute and chronic aerobic and resistance exercise: recent findings." Sports Med 2002;32(15):987-1004).

Wideman, Weltman, Patrie. (2000). "Synergy of L-arginine and GHRP-2 stimulation of growth hormone in men and women: modulation by exercise." Applied Journal of Physiology. Oct;279(4) R1467-77.

Widrick, (1996.) "Force-velocity and force- Power properties of single fiber from elite master runners and sedentary med." Am J Physiol. Aug;271 (2Pt 1):C676-83.

Winer, (1990). "Basal plasma growth hormone levels in man: new evidence for rhythmicity of growth hormone secretion." J Clin Endocrinology Metab. Jun;70(6):1678).

Weiss, EP (2006)."Lower extremity muscle size and strength and aerobic capacity decrease with caloric restriction but not with exercise-induced weight loss."J Appl Physiol).

Whyte LJ, (2010). "Effect of 2 weeks of sprint interval training on health-related outcomes in sedentary overweight/obese men." Metabolism. Oct;59(10):1421-8.).

Witzke, Snow. (2000). "Effects of plyometric jump training on bone mass in adolescent girls." Med Sci Sports Exerc. Jun;32(6):1051-7. PMID: 10862529.

Woynarowski, D. Fossel, Blackurn, (2011). "The Immortality Edge." (Wiley p.86-7).

Index

M

N

O

P

R

S

Hearing From You

*After doing this program for a couple of months my health improved dramatically, I am looking fabulous in comparison to before, the extra stubborn fat disappeared, I'm toned all around, I have way more energy, I could work non stop without sitting from early morning till bed time, I have no bone pain anymore and I'm much happier. **This is beyond amazing. I did not think that a form of exercise could do all these for you**. Thank you Phil!* - Diane Hornon

Next week will be week 14 on your program and I have told so many people about it I hope you sell a thousand copies. I am buying a copy for each of my sons right now. I am really impatient with the pace but I have lost 18 lbs and am possibly in the best shape of my life already at 55. I have only been able to do this because you defined how to do all this in such a short period of time. I can't thank you enough. - Craig Gilmore

Thank you for helping me achieve a level of fitness that I was beginning to think was unattainable. I am elated that I am able to participate with my four growing kids in their athletic adventures; Triathlons, gymnastics, running events, etc. You have no idea what level of hope and encouragement that you have given me, and give me daily, with your book, and your reports and articles contained on your web site. I tap into your material often. - Jeff

Another winner from Phil Campbell! This book and Sprint 8 helped me go from ZERO medals in 2015 to now 13 medals and counting in Masters Track and Field in 2016 alone. The exercises are never easy if you do them right but you definitely gets you results if you stick with it. Its a quick read and highly recommended for the weekend warrior to the professional athlete. - Derick

After not quite 3 months on your program, I've now burned about 19 pounds of fat, added about 4 pounds of muscle, and cut body fat by almost 6 percent. I'm tremendously grateful for your insights and am turning friends on to your book and ideas at every opportunity. I had a complete physical this morning and even my doctor was impressed. My cholesterol dropped 70 points (to 207 since my last test 2 years ago!!) I am stronger than I've ever been in my life and fitter than I've been in at least a decade. - Terry

Phil Campbell's newest book is in line with his other books. This version of the book breaks down the Sprint 8 and helps all readers to understand what to expect from workouts and post training information. I love the fact that he breaks down the intensity for heart rate and he even discuss the supplements needed to have that extra release of the Human Growth Hormone.
Phil keep up the great work!!!!!!! - Chris Morrison

Your book was a game changer for me. Good nutrition and your program along with some resistance training caused me to lose 100 pounds while putting on 20 pounds of muscle. - Michael Calder, age 55

I'm on week #11 of starting Sprint 8. So far I have lost 13 pounds, and I'm having no more tired slumps. I am noticing that my bottom recovery numbers are lower and better than when I started. My maximum intensity peaks have gone up. I noticed that the time my HR is in Fitness mode was 83 percent. The first week was 55 percent. My heart is getting stronger. Thanks Phil!
In Health from Taos, Claudia
 Claudia Bianca, MRET
Energy Healing Techniques
www.claudiabianca.com

*First of all, many thanks for your outstanding work. The E-Lifts and Sprint 8 workouts have revolutionized my fitness. I am 63, and **Sprint 8 has boosted my maximum heart rate from 162 to 171 in three months**. I have always been fit, but my maximum heart rate never went beyond 162 despite a full year of P90X, in addition to my martial arts workouts. Also, my waist has gone down by 1-2 inches even though I was a very lean guy to start with.*
I faithfully do Sprint 8 three times per week - usually mountain climbers, or the elliptical when I get to the gym. Initially, I could only do 45 mountain climbers (counting only the frequency of my right knee) in 30 seconds. Now, I can do 62 in 30 seconds, so I believe I'm adding fast twitch muscle fiber as you promised.
- Bill Stutesman, Plano, Texas

As an active cyclist as well as fitness enthusiast I am always looking for something to push me to the next level. I signed up for the Sprint 8 workshop held at my local bike shop (BGI Fitness). LOVED the program and book! I have incorporated it into my workout regimen. I am not a slave to the scale. I do periodically weigh myself, however, I go by how I feel, how my clothes look etc. I put on a pair of pants I hadn't worn in about a month and they were, well a bit loose. I jumped on the scale and in 2 weeks have lost 5 pounds. I am guessing inches as well! I LOVE the program and have encouraged others to jump on board! Thank You! Thank You! Thank You! THIS PROGRAM WORKS! Oh, and I can't wait to see how this translates to my increased speed and endurance on the bike! -- Kristen Schwark, Greenwood, IN

Sprint 8 workout was years ahead of its time

Blog by John Sadler -- *www.sadlersports.com*

For decades, the medical and fitness community touted slow and boring cardio. However, cardio has not proved to be beneficial for most adults when it comes to fat loss. But Phil was one of the first to promote his version of high intensity sprint interval training (Sprint 8) with the release of natural human growth hormone (HGH) and the associated health benefits including fat burning. In his book entitled: Ready, Set, GO!, SYNERGY FITNESS for Time-Crunched Adults, Phil explains the science behind his claims including documentation of the scientific tests. The original version was published in 2001 with the second edition being released in 2006. The book also introduced step by step instructions on his Sprint 8 workout. Phil's techniques have been publicized in O Oprah Magazine, Los Angeles Times, Outside Magazine, and Personal Fitness Professional as the fastest and most beneficial workout for busy adults.

Slow cardio dead, HIIT is better, but Sprint Interval is best. Slow cardio was the king for decades as its benefits were recommended by the American Heart Association and most health care professionals. But it has proven to not be an effective fat reducer and the workouts require a time commitment of at least 40 minutes. HIIT workouts (high intensity interval training), which went mainstream about five years ago, have exposed slow cardio and have proven to be a more effective alternative. But high intensity sprint interval workout are even more effective than HIIT. The sprints which can be completed in about 20 minutes with only 4 minutes dedicated to high intensity sprints, are much more intense and tests show that they release a much higher amount of HGH.

Phil's latest book entitled **Sprint 8 Cardio Protocol** outlines step by step how to implement sprint training on the track, in a pool, on a recumbent bicycle, and on an elliptical for maximum health benefits. It also provides a detailed scientific explanation of the changes that occur within the body during a high intensity sprint workout. My personal experience is that sprinting on an elliptical is more taxing than regular sprinting. Also, an elliptical also reduces the chances of a hamstring pull. - John Sadler (*https://www.sadlersports.com/blog/blogclient-profile-fitness-pioneer-phil-campbell-and-sprint-8-workout/*)